Worship Music
in the 21st Century

Worship Music
in the 21st Century

Selecting Proper Music for Worship in Regards to Lyrics, Instrumentation, and Rhythm

MARIUS E. MARTON

RESOURCE *Publications* • Eugene, Oregon

WORSHIP MUSIC IN THE 21ST CENTURY
Selecting Proper Music for Worship in Regards to Lyrics, Instrumentation, and Rhythm

Copyright © 2015 Marius E. Marton. All rights reserved. Except for brief quotations in critical publications or reviews, no part of this book may be reproduced in any manner without prior written permission from the publisher. Write: Permissions, Wipf and Stock Publishers, 199 W. 8th Ave., Suite 3, Eugene, OR 97401.

Resource Publications
An Imprint of Wipf and Stock Publishers
199 W. 8th Ave., Suite 3
Eugene, OR 97401

www.wipfandstock.com

ISBN 13: 978-1-4982-3104-6

Manufactured in the U.S.A.

Marika, my dearest wife, I dedicate this project to you. You have been by my side through this journey. Sometimes it was easy but most of the time it was hard. Due to deep research, many times I forgot what time it was and left you and our two amazing boys, Landen and Austin neglected.

Nonetheless, you continually encouraged me, gave me strength and the space I needed to work. You are my inspiration. Through this research I felt God inspiring me to write you a Love Song and our boys a Lullaby each. I loved you very much, but now I love you more.

Thank you for the sacrifice and your support. May God richly bless you for your kindness and for being a loving and supporting wife.

Contents

Foreword by Raj Attiken | ix
Acknowledgments | xi
Introduction | xiii

1 First Encounter with Music | 1
2 David, the Lyre Player | 12
3 Music as Evangelistic Tool | 19
4 Reacting to New Music | 29
5 A New Style is Born | 41
6 Theological Aesthetics | 51
7 The Power of Music | 64
8 Arguments | 73
9 Conclusion | 83

Bibliography | | 91

Foreword

ABOUT THREE YEARS AGO Marius E. Marton solicited my feedback on a project he was implementing for his Doctor of Ministry studies. I was aware of Marton's interest and professional training in music, and of his desire to develop a ministry that utilized music to mentor youth in his community. This book rises out of the work that Marton completed during this project and represents both his research and his personal insights.

Music is a central feature of Christian worship. This is true of liturgical worship, traditional evangelical worship, contemporary worship or emerging worship. Across the landscape of the Christian church there exists a vast array of musical forms, liturgies, and styles influenced by ethnic backgrounds, stylistic preferences and theological distinctions. Our current preferences have been subjected to historical processes that go back to the inception of the Christian church.

Music has for long been a controversial issue within the Christian community. Very few churches have spared of the music wars of recent decades. Some of them continue to bear the scars of intense battles; the trail of church splits is long. Churches make decisions about how they will worship. What they believe effects, determines, and shapes how they worship. And the way they worship effects what they believe. Music plays a key role in this ongoing process.

Marius E. Marton presents an essential treatise on an important and relevant topic for the Christian church. He points to

Foreword

biblical examples of positive and negative aspects of music, and reviews the role that music played in the life of David. Asserting that we do not see anywhere in Scripture that we are bound to a specific style or approach to music, Marton examines the purpose, potential, and credibility of various forms of worship music, and attempts to answer the criticisms leveled against different forms of music.

There is beauty, theology, and richness to what Marton describes regarding music that will be of value to those serious about communal worship. The book is a call to open our eyes and hearts to the variety of God-honoring music that is available to the Christian community today.

Raj Attiken, D.Min.,
Past President, Ohio Conference of Seventh-day Adventists
(1998–2014)

Acknowledgments

FIRST AND FOREMOST I want to express my deepest gratitude to God for the gift of music. My fascination with music began at a very early age in my childhood at home and church. This study is a result of that growing fascination. Among other marvelous creations of God music is one such creation that should be used to worship and praise its Creator.

Dr. Peter Bellini deserves special recognition for his wonderful mentorship, friendship, guidance and support through the journey of my dissertation project.

Dr. Emma Justes, dear professor and friend who taught me patiently to express my feelings through words and music.

Dr. Loris O. Chobanian, my guitar and composition professor at Baldwin-Wallace College Conservatory of Music, for believing in me and accepting me into the Conservatory of Music program.

My high school orchestra teacher, Fritz Schaufele, a special man who helped me reach new heights in the knowledge and performance of music.

My parents, Jacob and Maria, who forced me to learn piano even though I was tone-deaf when it came to music and Solfege.

Last but not least, my Church District I currently serve, Sandusky SDA Church and Norwalk SDA Church, where my music compositions, arrangements and performances are encouraged, welcomed and appreciated.

Introduction

As a pastor and musician I had the privilege to serve in different Evangelical and Protestant churches both as guest speaker and guest musician. It is always interesting to see how different churches choose different types of music for their worship. Some churches use the old fashioned pipe organ with a song leader trying to conduct or lead, others add a piano to play along the organ (although the piano is barely heard), other churches employ the help of a praise team to lead out in song service with the accompaniment of electric guitars, bass guitar, keyboard player and a drummer. It is also interesting to notice how members and/or visitors react to the use of music. I met people who condemn the use of electric and percussion instruments completely, while some people tolerate those instruments as long as they play softly and the good old southern gospels. Nothing contemporary is allowed, welcomed or tolerated because, well, they don't sound like the old songs. It was quite humorous to hear two elderly converse on the choice of sacred music. While both of them disliked contemporary music, one said that he preferred the church to sing the old hymns from the early 1800s, while the other did not want to go that far back, only to the 50s and 60s when Southern Gospel began to flourish. People have different opinions on what is proper sacred worship music, but the majority of people base their decisions on likes and dislikes instead of basing it on theological and musicological facts.

    This book does not seek to prove one or the other, but to open the reader's mind to consider contemporary music and different

INTRODUCTION

instrumentation in a new light. This book is not intended to promote contemporary music or contemporary instrumentation, but research has been done to see whether contemporary music is indeed harmful as some laymen claim, or could it be used in worship and be acceptable to God in a positive manner?

1

First Encounter with Music
The View of the Church Towards Worship Music

ROMANIA

JACOB AND MARIA MARTON was a young couple serving God in a communist country, Romania in the early seventies. The communist regime under the dictator Nicolae Ceausescu was very punitive towards Christianity. Many churches have closed their doors and ceased to gather for worship while other churches tried to fight the regime. There were others who simply took the church underground. The Seventh-day Adventist Church the Martons were attending decided to go underground. That meant to keep everything secret from the government. The treasurer had two books with financial records. One was the real book that only the pastor could have access to, and the other one was a fake book to show to government officials during their illicit visits. The church clerk also had two books. One book contained the real facts and church business issues and accurate church membership records, while the other contained fake information with limited details for the government's eyes. While the government pushed for atheism, the membership of this church in a small Transylvanian town flourished due to underground evangelization and secret baptisms during the dark hours of the night.

It was in the midst of this difficult time that Jacob and Maria had a baby boy. There was no name chosen because they were on vacation at the time, about a twelve-hour train ride from home. While the couple enjoyed the warm and sunny beaches of the Black Sea, I decided to be born. My parents were completely unprepared for my arrival. Although both my parents are of Hungarian descent, I was born in a part of the country where no Hungarian-speaking people lived, so the doctor pressured them into giving me a Romanian name. Thus, I got the name, Marius Eugene Marton.

Growing up under a communist regime was not easy. As children, we were constantly reminded not to talk to strangers, not to talk about politics or politicians on the street, and most of all, do not carry a Bible openly and do not talk about God openly in public. We were very cautious because it was estimated that about half of the citizens of Romania were snitching. There were snitches even in our church. I remember seeing men come to church on Sabbath morning in their work clothes because they spent the night at the police station being interrogated. These men would show the prints of their handcuffs on their wrists. I also remember my parents hiding musical instruments in our house from the secret police. My parents could afford to do that because my grandfather was among the wealthiest men in the town we lived in and our house was among the biggest at the time. Our house had the space to hide those musical instruments, Bibles and religious books, but our house was also a good choice because my parents were able to bribe government officials to look the other way. Everything was done by bribe during those times. The police chief promised my father to look the other way as long as they do not receive many reports from our snitching neighbors. So everything had to be done at night, in the dark and very quietly.

First Encounter with Music

Seeing all those instruments in the house and listening to the band arrangements in church, I was drawn to music early in my childhood. Seeing and having all those instruments in our house, gave me the opportunity to try each one whenever I desired. I remember being a small boy and trying to place a sousaphone around my neck, it was so funny because my tiny body could not reach the tubes to hold it on my shoulders, and the weight was too much for me. But I did not give up. I lay down and crawled into the sousaphone and tried to make sounds out of them. At that time every brass instrument was appealing to me; trumpet, flugelhorn French horn, trombone and tuba. I also remember playing German Blasmusik on those old vinyl discs while trying to play along on the instruments at hand. To this day my favorite is the Radetzky March by Johann Strauss Sr.

It was not long after the days of playing on those brass instruments that my parents hired a piano teacher for my older brother and me. I was only six years old when I began to learn to play the piano. The piano was a good choice, because it was an instrument that required no tuning expertise from the performer. I just had to push the right key at the right time and the right notes came out. The reason I was happy with the piano is because I had no musical ear at all, so if it would have been the violin for example or the trumpet, I could not tell whether I was playing the right note or if I was off tune. I fell in love with the piano and although at first my mother had to force me to practice, later it was a joy to play in church, home and school. I remember going to a piano recital competition where I played very well a Song Without Words by Felix Mendelsohn B., but was disqualified because it was not a piece written by a Romanian composer. The only style of music I was introduced to, as a child was Baroque, Classical and Romantic styles. The church used mostly hymns and cantatas of Bach. As I was enjoying these styles of music, at the age of ten I decided to become a professional musician with the dream to play in a symphony orchestra one day. But something happened at home.

One evening the police chief came to our house and informed my parents that they are coming within an hour to search our house. A snitching neighbor reported suspicious activity at our house and the police had to act on it. The courtesy heads-up was an hour notice. I can remember how fast my parents and fellow Christians carried the instruments and books out of our house through the back door. The police came and conducted a thorough search but found nothing. They took my parents to the station for questioning. Only my mother was released the next morning while my father was transported to another facility in another town. It took my mother days and much bribing to find out where my father was held. Only after bribing a very high ranking government official that my father was able to come home, but with a warning that a case is being prepared against him and his day in court will be soon. I remember one night sitting around the kitchen table with my family and seeing my parents deeply concerned about something. It was then that we, boys, found out that my father was about to risk his life trying to run across the border to Austria. We all knew well what happened to people that were caught running the border. Some were never seen again, while others, including a friend of my parents was beaten so bad by the secret police that when he got home, his wife did not recognize him. Once our father mentioned the possibility of living in a free country like Austria or West Germany, we were all on board for him to go. Little did we know at the time that my parents had to pay the sum of $10,000 to someone who promised to take my father all the way to Rome, Italy in a Mercedes-Benz. That someone took the money, but did not transport my father as promised. For three weeks we have not heard from our father. We prayed earnestly that God would be with him wherever he might be. After about three weeks our father called from a refugee camp in Austria. He never made it to Italy. He was caught at the Yugoslavian border and spent about a week at a refugee camp there, than tried again and successfully ran the border to Austria. There, he signed up for classes to learn about the American Government because that is where he was headed. Us boys were very happy to hear that we are moving to USA. Needless to say, my mother had to bribe several more government officials to help us obtain the visa faster and be able to have our family re-united at once. My father ran the Romanian border in 1985, and we, the rest of the family came to the States in June of 1987. If we would have known the future, perhaps the direction my parents chose would have been different, because only two years later, in 1989 communism fell in Romania and the dictator was executed along with his wife in December of the same year. At least we were together again. My father rented a small house in Lakewood, Ohio and attended the Hungarian Seventh-day Adventist Church in Westlake, Ohio. It was in this church that another chapter began in my life, not only spiritually but also musically.

United States of America

The pastor of that church came to our house weekly to prepare my older brother and me for baptism. My spiritual growth was delightful in this new church. In October of 1987 I was baptized by immersion into the body of Christ. It was a happy day for me. I accepted Jesus Christ as my personal Savior.

This church in Westlake had a good size group of young people and a church orchestra. While I enjoyed playing the piano and accompany my parents who were trained opera singers, I borrowed the church's cello and started playing it in the church orchestra. When I began my high school studies that summer at Lakewood High, the orchestra was so appealing to me that I signed up to play the cello there as well. It was like a dream come true. My musical ear was still weak, but I played softly and it was well received. At the church something else happened to me musically.

The young people there enjoyed singing as well and invited me to sing with them. I enjoyed their company and loved music, so I joined right of way. They sang new songs, not the old Bach hymns and cantatas I was used to back in Romania. The Review and Herald Publishing Association released a new compilation of songs, *He Is Our Song; The Music Collection for Youth*. It was a new style, new rhythms, and someone was strumming guitar chords instead of plucking with fingers. I was fascinated and drawn to these new songs.

Worship Music in the 21st Century

One Sabbath afternoon as I was standing by the piano with other young people and singing these songs, my mother came in quite furiously and marched right up to me, took the book out of my hand, slammed it on the pew and said, "We don't sing that kind of music." From that moment on I was forbidden to sing those songs at church and at home. Nobody asked me if I like those songs or if want to sing them, I was simply forbidden. When I am forbidden to do something, I do it anyway just to see what would I be missing had I obeyed. My parents had no idea that my musical talents have grown immensely during my high school years and the orchestra teacher was quite found of my musical talents. He asked me to play viola one year because there was a shortage of viola players and he thought of me to switch from cello to viola because in his opinion I was picking things up very fast. In my third and final year of high school I played classical guitar with him, performed Vivaldi's guitar concerto with the orchestra, played Pachelbel's Canon in D on harpsichord with the orchestra, but something else happened that my parents were not supposed to find out. I joined the jazz Roadshow.

The Jazz Roadshow was a jazz choir with a rhythm section. I played bass guitar in the rhythm section and loved it. If my parents had found out what I was doing, they would have punished me severely for playing what they called the devil's music.

Their definition of the devil's music confused me. They considered rock-n-roll as worldly and evil, but why contemporary church music also? Just because it did not sound like a hymn that Bach would write? They also considered guitar strumming a technique of the devil to lead young people away from the smoothing sound of acoustic instruments. Electric guitar and bass guitar fell in the same category. According to my parents, the drum set was an instrument invented by the devil himself to be used by those who want to worship the devil.

I never wanted to worship the devil, but at the same time, I never saw the devil when the Roadshow performed love songs and I played bass guitar. How could the devil show up in church when young people praise Jesus by singing contemporary songs?

First Encounter with Music

A struggle developed in my heart regarding the proper music for worship, but also for my personal enjoyment.

The dream to pursue a career in music never faded in my mind. With the help of my high school orchestra teacher I applied to Baldwin Wallace College Conservatory of Music in Berea, Ohio. Only one person believed in my being accepted into the program. Everyone else thought that I do not have a chance because the competition is too big and there were students way more prepared than I was. So I brought the matter before God.

After spending much time in prayer asking God to open the right doors and soften the hearts of people to accept me into the program, I decided to make my plea more appealing to God. So I offered up a deal that if God would help me get into the music program at Baldwin Wallace, I would use every opportunity to praise God's name with my musical talent. Lo and behold, it was in early spring, 1990, when I have received my acceptance letter from the Conservatory. It was a high day in my life. God opened the door and I was accepted; now it was my turn to keep up my end of the deal. However, the struggle still existed in my heart regarding proper music. I wanted to please and praise God, but at the same time, I enjoyed playing and listening to music that my parents labeled as satanic and evil. Some of the arguments did not make sense to me, while other arguments were far fetched and some of them did make some sense, but in my opinion was only applicable to very far out extremes.

Someone gave me a book by Jacob Aranza, *Backward Masking Unmasked*,[1] which seems detailed and authentic since Louisiana State Senator Bill Keith wrote the Introduction, but after reading it several times, it feels that Aranza is exposing the extreme side that did not draw me at all and was way too loud and scary for me at the time. One day I decided to give this book to my Music History professor and seek his opinion on the matter. I was completely surprised when he returned the book the next day and shared with

---

1. Jacob Aranza, *Backward Masking Unmasked; Backward Satanic Messages of Rock and Roll Exposed*, (Huntington House, Inc., Shreveport, Louisiana, 1984).

me his thoughts. Perhaps I should mention that Jacob Aranza was a minister at the time, and not a music critique and music specialist. The book he wrote analyzes the music of several rock groups and heavy metal groups based on his spiritual training and not as music expert.

Later another book ended up in my hands by Carol and Louis Torres, *Notes on Music*,[2] which analyzes music based on five components, (1) Melody, (2) Harmony, (3) Rhythm, (4) Tempo and (5) Tone color.[3] While Carol Torres was an accomplished violinist and played with the Long Island Symphony as concertmaster, Louis Torres serves as minister in the Seventh-day Adventist Church, neither are musicologists. Both Aranza and Torres analyze music from a spiritual point of view, but I was looking for a broader examination of music to find out which music is good and why. Spiritual arguments are not necessarily valid theological arguments. Spiritual arguments are mostly based on likes or dislikes or personal perceptions rather than facts and theological and musicological principles. Even when it comes to theological arguments, they in themselves are not sufficient for a holistic understanding, but a musicological argument is needed as well for a balanced view and complete analysis. Theological argument is one side of the coin and could easily be biased, so I turned to music experts for further answers and to find an equally balanced argument from both sides. After all, some of the arguments that people use from the spiritual or theological point of view, contradicts King David's counsel found in many of his psalms. For example let's look at Psalm 149:1–5, NRSV

> "Praise the Lord!
> Sing to the Lord a new song,
>   his praise in the assembly of the faithful.
> Let Israel be glad in its Maker;
>   let the children of Zion rejoice in their King.

---

2. Carol A. Torres & Louis R. Torres, *Notes on Music*, (LMN Publishing International, Inc., St. Maries, ID, *print date missing*).

3. Ibid., page 51, 52.

First Encounter with Music

Let them praise his name with dancing,
   making melody to him with tambourine and lyre.
For the Lord takes pleasure in his people;
   he adorns the humble with victory.
Let the faithful exult in glory;
   let them sing for joy on their couches."

The italics and bold letters were added for easier observation. David encourages people to sing new songs. If that is the case, why do my parents and some Christians want to sing hymns that were written by Bach or church pioneers in the 18th Century? As a composer, I was challenged several times by Christians wanting to know why I do not write music like Bach? Well, I am not Bach. If we look at the development of Western Music, Bach, yes, wrote beautiful hymns and cantatas and I love to listen to them, but if we compare Bach's successor's music to Bach's, it is very different. Mozart wrote in a new style. Mozart developed and built on the style of Bach and the Baroque music and developed his personal style, which we know as the Classical Period. Mozart's successor did not write music like Mozart, Beethoven wrote music in his own style, which we know as the Pre-Romantic Period. Beethoven did not write music in the style of Mozart, and so on. Music kept developing and changing in style. Today we love the music of Bach and Mozart and Beethoven and other great composers, but as the Composers Datebook program states on the local classical radio station, the announcer says it at the end of each presentation: "Reminding you that all music was once new." What we enjoy today as great music, it was not well received back when it was written. Is a song bad just because it is new?

David also encourages God's people to praise God with song and dance. How many Christians really practice song and dance? I remember growing up and singing in church or playing the piano, but was not allowed to sway my body back and forth or show any physical signs of enjoying the music. We had to stand like statutes and proclaim that we are happy with a long face.

Worship Music in the 21st Century

The instrumentation that David recommends in Psalm 149 is the tambourine and lyre. These are both instruments used in secular music settings during the Greek and Roman Empire. That concept goes beyond the notion that only classical music is good and all other is bad. The tambourine is not a lyrical instrument like the violin or trumpet, but simply a percussion instrument. David lived long before the Greek and Roman Empire, yet recommends us to use these instruments in our worship and our worship ought to be joyful and loud. Let's look at Psalm 150, NRSV:

> "Praise the Lord!
> Praise God in his sanctuary;
>   praise him in his mighty firmament!
> Praise him for his mighty deeds;
>   praise him according to his surpassing greatness!
> Praise him with trumpet sound;
>   praise him with lute and harp!
> Praise him with tambourine and dance;
>   praise him with strings and pipe!
> Praise him with clanging cymbals;
>   praise him with loud clashing cymbals!
> Let everything that breathes praise the Lord!
> Praise the Lord!"

Another example where David recommends tambourine and dance with the trumpet and harp and strings and pipe, but now includes clanging cymbals and loud clashing cymbals in worship. Reading these psalms and others on one hand and listening to my parents' reasoning on the other hand, the confusion was strong. While David recommends us to be open and genuine in our worship, I was taught to be boxed in, limited and inexpressive. I wanted answers. Not just one sided answers, but theological, doctrinal, theoretical and musicological answers.

Today, as a professional composer, conductor and performer and an ordained minister of the Gospel in the Seventh-day Adventist Church, I encountered questions in regard to sacred worship

First Encounter with Music

music everywhere I served as a speaker, pastor or visitor. In order to find questions, I have decided to do a Doctoral Dissertation on this topic and see the entire picture without a biased impression. The idea is not to condone one side and condemn the other, but to be fair to both sides and give equal opportunity for arguments. The desired outcome is similar to David's desire: Praise the Lord!

2

David, the Lyre Player
The Effects of Good Music vs. Bad Music in the Old Testament

MUSIC PLAYED AN IMPORTANT role in the history of the Israelites throughout the Old Testament. Its existence and use is evident from the book of Genesis when the father of musicians, Jubal, is mentioned (Genesis 4:21). In Old Testament times, the biblical community was aware of the effects of music on the human mind. In this chapter, a passage from 1 Samuel is examined to show the knowledge they possessed back then about the effects of music, which is confirmed by modern day musical therapists and musicologists.

The Old Testament passage that is examined is 1 Samuel 16:14–23:

> "Now the spirit of the Lord departed from Saul, and an evil spirit from the Lord tormented him. And Saul's servants said to him, "See now, an evil spirit from God is tormenting you. Let our lord now command the servants who attend you to look for someone who is skillful in playing the lyre; and when the evil spirit from God is upon you, he will play it, and you will feel better." So Saul

DAVID, THE LYRE PLAYER

said to his servants, "Provide for me someone who can play well, and bring him to me." One of the young men answered, "I have seen a son of Jesse the Bethlehemite who is skillful in playing, a man of valor, a warrior, prudent in speech, and a man of good presence; and the Lord is with him." So Saul sent messengers to Jesse, and said, "Send me your son David who is with the sheep." Jesse took a donkey loaded with bread, a skin of wine, and a kid, and sent them by his son David to Saul. And David came to Saul, and entered his service. Saul loved him greatly, and he became his armor-bearer. Saul sent to Jesse, saying, "Let David remain in my service, for he has found favor in my sight."

And whenever the evil spirit from God came upon Saul, David took the lyre and played it with his hand, and Saul would be relieved and feel better, and the evil spirit would depart from him."[1]

In this story, the author of the book of Samuel not only informs the reader of the power and influence music has on the human brain, but also introduces God's providence as David is introduced to Saul and to royal lifestyle in preparation of his future calling. The Bible records other situations where God uses unexpected methods to accomplish something. For example, Joseph's tragic youthful years which are spent in slavery and prison in a foreign country away from his family. Joseph could have rebelled against God, and rightly so, for his fate. Instead, according to Genesis 45:4–8, he realizes God has a plan all along to preserve his family by allowing his brothers to sell him to Egyptians. "Then Joseph [says] to his brothers, '"Come closer to me." And they went closer. He [says], 'I am your brother, Joseph, whom you sold into Egypt. And now do not be distressed, or angry with yourselves, because you sold me here, for God sent me before you to preserve life. For the famine has been in the land these two years; and there are five more years in which there will be neither plowing nor harvest. God sent me before you to preserve for you a remnant on earth, and to keep alive for you many survivors. So it was not you

---

1. 1 Samuel 16:14–23 NRSV.

who sent me here, but God; he has made me a father to Pharaoh, and lord of all his house and ruler over all the land of Egypt.'" God uses Joseph's suffering to preserve life according to Genesis, and according to the passage in 1 Samuel. God uses Saul's suffering to prepare David for his calling. In addition, it is quite remarkable that God uses one's musical talent to bring healing and wholeness to a person's life as well.

The passage in Samuel begins with the sad news that the spirit of the Lord has departed from Saul. That the Lord's spirit has departed from Saul means it had to have come upon him first. In the same book, there is a description of Saul's anointing by the prophet Samuel and the promise that Samuel makes to him. As is recorded in 1 Samuel 10:6, Samuel tells Saul, "Then the spirit of the Lord will possess you, and you will be in a prophetic frenzy along with them and be turned into a different person." The spirit of the Lord is upon Saul at the beginning of his calling, but in this passage it is recorded that the same spirit departs from Saul. When the spirit of the Lord is upon Saul, he is able to discern divine prophecy from human ambition. In his spirit-filled state, Saul is humble and consults with the prophet about his decisions. He does not act without God telling him where to go.

When the spirit of the Lord is not present, there is room for the enemy's influence to overshadow God's guidance. This passage describes the appearance of an evil spirit from the Lord. This raises questions about whether God works in collaboration with evil spirits, or whether evil simply finds its way in in the absence of God's spirit? In either case, it is obvious there is a difference in Saul's behavior and mentality because the new spirit torments him. Saul's servants believe the evil spirit has come from God. However, in an Old Testament worldview, everything has come from God, good or bad. The author of the book of Job makes the same interpretation when Job is tortured. His own friends think God is punishing him for secret sins. The author makes it clear that Satan is tormenting him and not God. God does allow Job to be tested and proved. Perhaps, the same thing is going on with Saul. People assume it is God, but, in essence, it is most likely Satan

David, the Lyre Player

tormenting Saul. In the New Testament in James 1:17, James asserts, "Every generous act of giving, with every perfect gift, is from above, coming down from the Father of lights, with whom there is no variation or shadow due to change." Theologically, this understanding of God as the generous giver of every perfect gift stands in opposition to the idea that God allows bad things to happen to us and even goes as far as to give Satan permission to torment us. For believers, there is a great deal of tension in this 1 Samuel text surrounding the tormenting spirit that is not easy to resolve.

When the spirit of the Lord leaves Saul, he becomes a completely different person. He no longer listens to the voice of God through the prophet, but acts on his own ambition and pride. Humility is also gone. He becomes angry and violent. His anger and violent state become so aggressive that his own servants request a hired musician to come and play sacred music in order to bring back the spirit of the Lord.

Saul's servants prove to be wise as they suggest for him to seek out someone who is skillful in playing the lyre, a musical instrument. During this time, there are only two known stringed instruments, the *kinnor* lyre and the *nebel*. "In the English versions of the Old Testament the former word is wrongly translated "harp." In both instruments the strings were set in vibration by the fingers, or perhaps by a little stick, the plectrum (as Josephus says). Bow instruments were unknown to the ancients. The strings were made of gut, metal strings were not used in olden times."[2] Unfortunately, there is no musical notation preserved from this time, so we do not know what the melody or music sounded like when David played the lyre; however we do know that the most common lyres of the time had anywhere from three-eight strings.

Although it is hard to imagine a melodic line or chord progression being played on such an instrument, the story maintains that David is a skillful player. This old Jewish coin of Bar Kokba,

---

2. T. K. Cheyne and J. Sutherland Black, ed., *Encyclopaedia Biblica, Volume III* (New York: MacMillan Company, 1899), 298.

15

Old Israel 25 Argarot Coin[3] shows a three stringed lyre. There is no evidence as to how the three strings would have been tuned.

There is most likely not a lot of flexibility for high tuning since the strings would have been made of gut. The skill in playing such an instrument is easily debatable in comparison to a six or twelve string guitar with a fingerboard. Whether the lyre contains three or eight strings, it is not comparable to the modern guitar. The modern guitar has a fingerboard for the player to produce different notes or chords of a key, while the lyre does not have a fingerboard for different notes and ranges. The method of playing the lyre is either by plucking the strings or by using a plectrum to accompany the singer. All of this simply leads to a lot speculation what David is able to play with such limitations. However, the biblical witness is clear that David knows how to use what he has in a way that is a blessing and pleasant to the ear.

Saul's servants know that when this instrument is played skillfully, the evil spirit will depart. This indicates that they have some form of knowledge about the power of music. Saul does not hesitate but sends the servants out to find this skillful player. When one servant speaks up regarding David, he not only knows of his musical talents, but also gives an entire resume of his other talents and abilities. The most important thing David has on his side as the servant tells Saul is the Lord's presence.

This passage captures David out with the sheep when the servants arrive at his father's house. The young David has plenty of time to master the art of the lyre as he spends his days out in the field tending to sheep. It is fascinating that David masters the lyre in particular. There is no mention of any other instrument. This is fascinating because the lyre is used at joyous public festivities, processions and other festivities at home. The Old Testament mentions other musical instruments that are associated with religious rituals only. The lyre is the instrument used for these joyous

---

3. "Old Israel 25 ARGOROT Coin," Delcampe.net, accessed on March 5, 2014, http://www.delcampe.net/page/item/id,164856680,var,Old-israel-25-AGOROT-Coin-Ancient-judaica-write-ARAB-HEBREW-Three-stringed-lyre,language,E.html.

DAVID, THE LYRE PLAYER

festivities and to accompany psalms. This instrument is small enough and shaped in such a way that the player can play it even while walking. David's mastery of this instrument supports his authorship of the psalms and his love for joyous music. He is either too young or does not have access to the *nebel*, which is only used in Temple services and religious rituals. Since Saul needs joyous music, a skilled lyre player is the best choice.

Jesse, David's father does not hesitate to comply with the king's request. Immediately, Jesse sends David on his way with a donkey loaded with bread, a skin of wine, and a kid. When David comes to Saul, the first impression is positive. The Scripture points out that David enters Saul's service and is greatly loved by the king. David not only plays the lyre for Saul, but also becomes his armor bearer as well. After Saul accepts David into his service, he sends a message to Jesse and asks for his permission for David to remain there. David finds favor in the eyes of the king.

Saul knows he is the first king of Israel chosen by God. He is supposed to be filled by the spirit of the Lord to lead the nation to God. "Unlike Saul, David is given no signs and no initial commission to fulfill, yet the divine ordering or circumstances is as apparent in his case as in Saul's; ironically, his first task as the Lord's anointed is to serve the existing king."[4] Apparently, Saul struggles with his status as personal ambition and being a humble king to serve God.

From that moment on, David is on call at all times. Whenever Saul feels tormented by the evil spirit, David begins to play his lyre. Perhaps, this is a dream come true for David. It is obvious he enjoys playing the lyre since he has mastered the instrument on his own while out in the fields. When David arrives at Saul's court, he is getting paid to do what he loves, and a miracle happens when David plays his lyre. The great effect comes either from David's talent or the fact that the Lord is with him.

Saul, who is tormented by an evil spirit, is relieved and feels better, and the evil spirit departs from him. Music has a special

---

4. Catherine Clark Kroeger and Mary J. Evans, ed., *The IVP Women's Bible Commentary* (Downers Grove: Inter Varsity Press, 2002), 164.

power. However, it has a greater influence when the Lord is with the musician. Although this treatment is good, it is only a temporary solution. Later, in 1 Samuel 18:10, 11, Saul's rage is described as it overtakes the power of David's music, "The next day an evil spirit from God rushes upon Saul, and he raves within his house, while David is playing the lyre, as he does day by day. Saul has his spear in his hand; and Saul throws the spear, for he thinks, 'I will pin David to the wall.' But David eludes him twice." Once again, the passage shows how angry and violent Saul is when the spirit of the Lord departs from him. Consequently, music is a powerful tool, but, based on this story, it becomes more powerful if it is accompanied by the Lord's presence. I heard so many wonderful Christians fear the effects of satanic music, but if we listen to Godly music, we not only have nothing to fear, but receive a much mightier effect of divine origin that helps improve our health, our imagination, our blood flow in our bodies, calm the stressed and spark creativity in the brain. According to Kim Lawson,[5] if you listen to music every day, you have a lesser chance of suffering with Alzheimer's disease. Music definitely has good benefits. I choose my music selection carefully for my listening pleasure because I want to be the recipient of good benefits and not the destructive benefits.

---

5. Dr. Kim Lawson, *Ministry with People with Disabilities; Emphasis on Alzheimer's Disease,*" (lecture given at United Theological Seminary Intensive Week, Dayton, OH, January 31, 2015).

3

Music as Evangelistic Tool
Art is God's Gift to Describe Divine Beauty

THERE ARE MANY EVANGELISTS preaching the Gospel in tents, buildings, churches, under the open sky, online, TV, radio, facebook and every other imaginable venue they are able to use to draw people to Christ. I was one of those evangelists traveling for eleven years as a self-supporting evangelist preaching the good news of the Gospel in three languages.

It was a joy seeing people accept Jesus Christ as their personal Savior and give their hearts to Him through the symbolic act of baptism. However, as I look back and contemplate on those wonderful memories I have collected in over forty five evangelistic series I have held, the majority of people who accepted Christ as their personal Savior were either married couple, middle aged people and elderly. Very few young people were drawn to Jesus through those evangelistic series. Unfortunately as a beginner and young evangelist I did not have the tools, knowledge and courage to change my techniques to reach young people as well. Today, I use music as a tool for evangelism. The majority of young people love music, whether it is by playing a musical instrument, singing or listening to on their iPod or iPhones. Why not use music to reach young people and introduce Jesus to them through the beauty of music? The right lyrics on a beautiful melody accompanied by wonderful chord progressions and impressive instrumental solos may help young people develop a relationship with Christ. When I say young people, I refer to teenagers and pre-teens that are exposed to music at their local church or school and appreciate the art.

Let's examine a New Testament passage where Jesus tells the disciples to allow little children come to Him from the Gospel of Matthew 19:13–15,

> "Then little children [are] being brought to him in order that he might lay his hands on them and pray. The disciples [speak] sternly to those who brought them; but Jesus [says], "Let the little children come to me, and do not stop them; for it is to such as these that the kingdom of heaven belongs." And he [lays] his hands on them and [goes] on his way."[1]

This particular passage does not mention the use of music at all. It does not make mention of people singing who bring little children to Jesus, or of the children singing as they are being brought, music does not appear at all. This particular passage has been chosen because the context of this project deals with bringing children and young people to Jesus. The argument has been made that music can be used by God as an evangelical tool. Now, the emphasis of this New Testament passage is to prove Jesus has room for children and young adults. In fact, this passage corroborates that Jesus' desire is for children to be introduced to Him at a very early age in order to develop a solid relationship with him as they mature. In this context, music makes this relationship sweeter and stronger.

Matthew does not specify who is bringing little children to Jesus. That is not of importance. It could have been mothers, fathers, grandparents or legal guardians. It could have been neighbors, relatives, friends, coworkers, synagogue members or

---

1. Matthew 19:13–15 NRSV.

synagogue leaders. Ultimately, it does not matter who brings them. The important part is that children are brought to Jesus, and that those involved in this process see the importance of bringing little children to Jesus.

In earlier passages of Matthew, Jesus discusses and offers his divine interpretation on family and its importance. Jesus makes it a point that family is important and children are part of this nucleus. They are not to be ignored or pushed aside. According to David L. Turner, Jesus "welcomes [children]. Jesus' affirmation of and care for children provide an important model for his disciples."[2] Jesus calls for children. The disciples learn a very important lesson here; invite and welcome children to Christ Jesus. According to Turner, children are believers who are to be trained as disciples for Jesus.

The other factor Matthew does not specify is the age of the little children indicating that the exact age does not matter either. The little children must be under teenage years, or they would not be referred to as such. Also, they could be as young as infants or toddlers.

People, parents and legal guardians need to be trained and exposed to the benefits and blessings of bringing little children to Jesus at an early age. Matthew not only records that people bring little children to Jesus, but also clarifies the purpose of their being brought. They want Jesus to lay his hands on them and pray. The laying on of hands in those days means, "to impart a blessing."[3] Jesus blesses adults as he travels from town to town, but these people want little children to be blessed as well. This petition or request is not a new one. According to the Law of Moses, newborns are brought before the priest when they are forty days old to be presented to God in the purification process of the mother as described in Leviticus 12. Jesus himself is presented in the Temple as the Gospel of Luke describes in 2:22–24, "When the time came for their purification according to the law of Moses, they brought him

---

2. David L. Turner, *Matthew: Baker Exegetical Commentary on the New Testament* (Grand Rapids: Baker Publishing Group, 2008), 464.

3. Harold Attridge, ed., *The Harper Collins Study Bible: Fully Revised and Updated NRSV* (San Francisco: Harper Collins Publishers, 2006), 1701.

up to Jerusalem to present him to the Lord (as it is written in the law of the Lord, 'Every firstborn male shall be designated as holy to the Lord'), and they offered a sacrifice according to what is stated in the law of the Lord, "a pair of turtledoves or two young pigeons."

The little children in our passage are probably older than forty days, and most likely have been taken to the priest according to their laws; therefore, this blessing pronounced by Jesus and his prayer for them is special. This approach of the people challenges the mentality of the time regarding the practice of laying on of hands because that practice is reserved for special times such as when someone is chosen to fulfill an office in New Testament church setting. The fact that little children are brought to Jesus extends this practice beyond cultural norms and local expectation. Therefore, it is no surprise that the disciples speak 'sternly' to the people. R.T. France goes a step further as he talks about "welcoming a child in the name of Jesus. Children matter in the kingdom of heaven. But the gesture [laying on of hands] is also appropriate for commissioning someone for a special responsibility."[4] According to France, children are to be trained to be responsible in divine matters and need to be commissioned as such.

According to the Webster Merriam Dictionary "stern" as an adjective means either "1 a: having a definite hardness or severity of nature or manner: AUSTERE; b: expressive of severe displeasure: HARSH; 2: forbidding or gloomy in appearance."[5]

The disciples are not always gentle, nice or compassionate. On the contrary, they use a harsh tone of voice and words as they send people away. The Bible does not specify whether this mistake is theological or practical. However, it is obvious that Jesus cares about children so much that their action to send them away is an insult. The disciples take matters into their own hands instead of asking their master whether he wants to lay hands on children.

---

4. R.T. France, *The Gospel of Matthew: The New International Commentary on the New Testament* (Grand Rapids: William B. Eerdmans Publishing Company, 2007), 727.

5. "Stern," Miriam-Webster, www.merriam-webster.com/dictionary/stem (accessed on 28 February 2013).

After this, they learn an important lesson from Jesus to show compassion and be merciful to the children.

From the perspective of the adults bringing their children who are initially turned away, one can imagine the disappointment those people felt at that moment. The Scripture does not specify the distance from whence they came. Perhaps, some are locals, while others come from neighboring towns, since it is not unusual for people to travel to another town to see and hear Jesus or be healed by him. Perhaps, they are discouraged by the disciples' harsh words and actions. The good news is that Jesus embraces them. The people leave encouraged and transformed by this holy encounter.

In his wisdom, Jesus reacts right away and interrupts the disciples before they have the chance to actually send the people away. One can almost hear Jesus' quick response saying, "Let the little children come to me, and do not stop them." This statement shows that Jesus wants to spend time with the little children. Donald A. Hagner breaks down this Biblical passage into four parts, "(1) the presentation of little children for blessing; (2) the disciples' objection; (3) Jesus' affirmation of the children, consisting of (a) the invitation and (b) the grounds for the invitation; and (4) the blessing and Jesus' departure."[6] They must have been embarrassed as Jesus reprimands them in front of all those bystanders. Then, Jesus adds the second part of His statement, "For it is to such as these that the kingdom of heaven belongs." Jesus makes it clear that the kingdom of heaven belongs to those who are like little children. This statement can be interpreted in two ways, literally and symbolically. The literal interpretation concludes that children have access to heaven just like any adult; therefore nobody should stop them from coming or from being brought. The symbolic interpretation is broader and it refers to "those of humble status."[7] In symbolic language, this group represents all those who cannot

---

6. Donald A. Hagner, *Word Biblical Commentary, Volume 33b: Matthew 14–28* (Nelson Reference & Electronic: A Division of Thomas Nelson Publishers, 1995), 552.

7. Attridge, *The Harper Collins Study Bible*, 1701.

come by themselves but need assistance to be brought to Jesus. It refers to those who are lost and cannot find the way (see the parable of the lost sheep in Matthew 18, or the lost coin and the prodigal son in Luke 15). So, basically, it refers to everyone in the world. After reprimanding the disciples and sharing a teaching, Jesus lays his hands on the children. This must have been a sight to see for everyone. According to Hagner, "Jesus' response must have surprised the disciples, for he emphatically invites the little children to come to him. If little children are a model for disciples, then they obviously have their proper place in the presence of Jesus."[8] This is a new deed of Jesus that is not practiced until this time. One can only imagine the joy and fulfillment the people must feel for Jesus' response to their little children.

The same scenario is recorded in the Gospel of Mark as well in 10:13–16. However, Mark adds that Jesus is indignant. The Merriam Webster's Dictionary defines the word indignant in adjective form as "feeling or showing anger because of something unjust or unworthy."[9] According to Mark, Jesus is not pleased by the way his disciples handle the situation. Jesus even shows anger because the little children are rejected. That again emphasizes the important place children have in Jesus' heart. If Jesus is indignant towards such action, the church today ought to have the same reaction when people, young adults or children are turned away.

Mark goes on to describe the words of Jesus to his disciples in verse 15, "Truly I tell you, whoever does not receive the kingdom of God as a little child will never enter it." The emphasis is on the willingness to receive as a little child. The little children who seem unworthy in the eyes of his disciples become the center of his lesson. Adults must learn from these little children; the children are willing to come and allow themselves to be brought to Jesus without hesitation or murmuring. Michael J. Wilkins points out, "Jesus' gentle openness to them, his compassionate touch, and his protective words elevate them from being marginally irrelevant to

---

8. Hagner, *Word Biblical Commentary*, 553.

9. "Indignant," Miriam-Webster, www.merriam-webster.com/dictionary/indignant (accessed on 28 February 2013).

being valuable objects of his gospel outreach."[10] Jesus lifts up those whom seem insignificant in their current society and culture as important. Jesus reverses the cultural norms.

Mark adds another detail Matthew does not record. In Mark 10:16, it is recorded "And he took them up in his arms, laid his hands on them, and blessed them." Matthew did not record the fact that Jesus takes them up in his arms. This shows an added level of intimacy and connection that Jesus shares with the children. If the children are really small, from infancy to toddler age, they may not have understood the words or actions of Jesus, but it must have been wonderful for the adults. Like children, adults do not need to understand everything that is said or happening around them as long as Jesus is in charge. This dynamic makes it even more challenging for adults to receive the kingdom of God like the little children. Jesus does not leave the people with an easy charge, but with a charge that is worthy to pursue.

This story is in all of the synoptic Gospels: Luke also records this event. The passage is found in Luke 18:15–17. While Matthew and Mark specify little children being brought to Jesus, Luke uses the word "infants." The Webster Merriam Dictionary defines infant and child differently. Merriam Webster Dictionary refers to children as "a child in the first period of life, a person who is not of full age."[11] While infant is defined in the same dictionary as "an unborn or recently born person."[12] Based on these two definitions, it can still be concluded that the little children are very young.

The disciples should already know Jesus' way of dealing with children and the special attention he shows them. Some commentary on this passage explains, "*sternly ordered*, lit. 'rebuked.'"[13] At this moment, the disciples agree on rebuking the people. This is

---

10. Michael J. Wilkins, *The NIV Application Commentary: Matthew* (Grand Rapids: Zondervan, 2004), 646.

11. "Infant," Miriam-Webster, accessed on February 28, 2013, www.merriam-webster.com/dictionary/infant (accessed on 28 February 2013).

12. "Child," Miriam-Webster, accessed on February 28, 2013, www.merriam-webster.com/dictionary/child (accessed on 28 February 2013).

13. Attridge, *The Harper Collins Study Bible*, 1798.

happening in the church today where people wanting to do something for Jesus are rebuked by unconverted disciples. The word unconverted is being introduced because Jesus' disciples have already had an encounter with a child earlier. In the Gospel of Luke 9:46–48, Luke records that, "An argument arose among them as to which one of them was the greatest. But Jesus, aware of their inner thoughts, took a little child and put it by his side, and said to them, 'Whoever welcomes this child in my name welcomes me, and whoever welcomes me welcomes the one who sent me; for the least among all of you is the greatest.'" Jesus has already taught them to become like little children. Apparently, the lesson has not been learned. Most likely, they have a different interpretation of Jesus' words just as many today interpret it differently as well. A child is presented before them then, and now several children are being brought to Jesus. The disciples, and believers today, should get the picture of how important children are to Jesus after the second incident.

Even though Jesus has taught a lesson on humility and childlike character, the main text of Matthew 19, Mark 10 and Luke 18 all record a new scenario where Jesus is teaching the very same lesson to his disciples. Praise God for his patience toward the slow learning adults!

The study notes under the Luke 9 passage add another crucial detail for adults to consider, "the qualities of openness, low status, and no claim to achievement characterize the *little child*."[14] The emphasis is placed on the latter part of that statement, "no claim to achievement." Where adults boast about personal achievement and make the connection of their worthiness based on those achievements, little children do not do this. Very young children are not even concerned about their achievements. With this insight, believers learn a very important lesson about the Kingdom of God, that it is not based on merit or personal achievement, but on humility and quality of openness.

According to John Nolland, "Jesus will draw the children into the coming of the blessings of the kingdom of heaven in his own

14. Ibid., 1799.

ministry."[15] Nolland continues to argue that the early church faced some problems regarding the use of children in worship or what to do with them at all. Through Jesus' example, we also get a sense of children's unique contribution to ministry. When Jesus made his point clear and taught the lesson, his prayer "brings closure to the account."[16]

As children are attracted to music, it is a great tool to use in drawing them to Jesus and to praise him through this art. Time ought to be dedicated to training children and welcoming them to Christ. First, Jesus rebuked those who hinder the children from coming to him. Then, he takes time for the children by inviting them to himself. Music projects ought to reach out to those who hinder teenagers and pre-teens from coming to Jesus. It is there that they ought to hear the invitation to come to Jesus through the beauty and art of music. When pre-teens and teenagers respond to that invitation, time is taken to train them, educate them, and introduce them to Jesus to receive a divine blessing. These children are trained to play musical instruments and are prepared for church concert events and worship music.

In the example of David, God uses music as a ministry tool and a way for the young shepherd to earn a living in the royal court and to bring healing to the king's ailments. In the example of the disciples, Jesus uses little children to teach them about the importance of humility and the quality of openness. Based on the two main New Testament passages, it can be deduced that music is an effective tool to introduce Jesus to children and draw them to him. Based on the Old Testament Scripture, sacred music not only draws people to God, but also has a positive effect on them because the lyrics of sacred songs focus on the goodness and mercy of God and the love God has for us, humans. That hope and joy is expressed in different types of musical styles with different instrumentation based on the local culture. While one melody uplifts the people in one culture, the same melody may not have similar

---

15. John Nolland, *The Gospel of Matthew; A Commentary on the Greek Text* (Grand Rapids: William B. Eerdmans Publishing Company, 2005), 784.

16. Ibid., 785.

effects in a different culture. People ought to be free to express the joy they have in God in a melody, harmony, chord progression, rhythm and instrumentation that uplifts their soul to heaven and helps them go through their struggles and business of daily life.

That is why I like to write my own songs because the words and the components that make up the song reflect on my emotions at the time. That is why David wrote the Psalms, because those are his testimonies and personal feelings. I encourage everyone to write their own songs and make up their own melodies to fit the situation and experience they are feeling at the time. When I studied at the Conservatory, my professors instructed me to learn as much as possible about the piece I am playing and the composer that wrote it. That way I can get into the shoes of the composer and portray his/her feelings when that particular piece was composed. That is fine up to point. When I play Beethoven, I want to know what he felt when he wrote that piece, but I do not want to live my life in other peoples' shoes all the time. I want to express my own feelings my own way. Music is a wonderful art that can help me make this happen. David wrote Psalms, I write my own music and I encourage you, the reader, to express your feelings through music, your way. Do not be influenced by anybody or anything, express to God what you feel through your own song or musical instrument. It may just be a rewarding revelation and peace to be able to express self freely to God and sing praises all day long.

4

Reacting to New Music
How the Church Reacted to New Music in History

THROUGHOUT HISTORY, THE CHURCH was in tension with popular music. In light of this tension, the church was even against sacred music that encompassed sacred instrumentation with sacred words but was in the style of secular compositions. However, much to the church's displeasure, it was this type of music that composers experimented with and reformers promoted, i.e. a hybrid of secular music with sacred lyrics. As popular music changed over time, sacred music challenged Christian leaders by bringing this new style into the church. In this chapter, several historical events will be analyzed to show how composers and reformers influenced this shift in sacred music and how the church reacted to them.

One of the oldest preserved songs is housed in the National Museum of Copenhagen. The title of this song is *Epitaph of Seikilos*. "It is one of the few surviving examples of Greek music. It is inscribed on the tomb of Seikilos (2nd or 1st century B.C.) at Tralles in Asia Minor."[1] This example is mentioned to show the

---

1. J.A. Westrup and F.L.I. Harrison, *The New College Encyclopedia of Music* (New York: W.W. Norton & Company, Inc., 1981), 494.

simplicity of ancient music, scale, harmony, lyrics, notation and rhythm. There is no melodic scale or key. Instead, modes are used. The rhythm is not a strict pattern and there is no harmony. One melodic line with arbitrary note progressions makes up this short composition. The lyrics translated from Greek are "As long as you live, be lighthearted. Let nothing trouble you. Life is only too short, and time takes its toll."[2] These lyrics are neither religious nor secular, but supposedly it is a song of a husband to his deceased wife. It is pretty evident that this is a simple song.

Two instruments were used in Greek music, the *aulos* and the *lyre*. The *aulos* was "a double-reed instrument, the most important wind instrument of the ancient Greeks."[3] The *lyre* was the "instrument of the ancient Greeks, Assyrians, and Hebrews. It was a simpler form of *kithara*, having a body made of tortoise shell or wood, and two horns or wooden arms joined by a cross bar; it had the same number of strings, varying from three to twelve."[4] The Greeks regarded music as being of divine origin and a gift to humankind. According to Greek mythology, the earliest "practitioners were gods and demigods, such as Apollo, Amphion, and Orpheus."[5] Plato, the Greek philosopher, wrote in his book, *The Republic*, to Benjamin Jowett stating, "Music gives a soul to the universe, wings to the mind, flight to the imagination and life to everything."[6] According to Greek mythology, "music had magic powers: people thought it could heal sickness, purify the body and mind, and work miracles in the realm of nature."[7] Both Plato and Socrates agreed that only mentally well-balanced students should be taught the art of music. If the student is mentally ill, his art

---

2. Claude V. Palisca, *Norton Anthology of Western Music*, 4th ed. (New York: W.W. Norton & Company, Inc., 2001), 1.

3. Westrup and Harrison, *The New College Encyclopedia of Music*, 47.

4. Ibid., 333.

5. Donald Jay Grout and Claude V. Palisca, *A History of Western Music*, 4th ed. (New York: W.W. Norton & Company, 1988), 23.

6. Benjamin Jowett, *The Republic of Plato, Book III* (Oxford: Clarendon Press, 1888), 88.

7. Grout and Palisca, *A History of Western Music*, 3.

will cause his hearers to be ill as well, but the mentally healthy student will have healthy influence on his hearers.[8] Music directly imitates the passions or states of the soul . . . when one listens to music that imitates a certain passion, he becomes imbued with the same passion; and if over a long time he habitually listens to music that rouses ignoble passions, his whole character will be shaped to an ignoble form.[9] They realized music could be beneficial but also dangerous. Even though music was primarily used in worship, whether worshipping God or Baal, nature, love or beauty, good music played by mentally ill performers could subconsciously lead listeners into a mentally ill state where the mind could be controlled against the will of the listener. These beliefs about the power of music to influence a person's mental and/or moral state were taken very seriously.

Ancient Rome had taken the art of music from Greece; however, they began to alter the instruments. "The Roman version of the *aulos, tibia,* occupied an important place in religious rites, military music, and the theater. Several brass instruments were prominent."[10] The *lyre* developed into harp, *viola de gamba,* violoncello, double bass, viola and violin. From the *aulos* evolved the recorder, flute, oboe, clarinet and bassoon. "From the valveless brass instruments came three-valve instruments that could produce sound in every key and fast chromatic scales. Those brass instruments that were born during the Roman Empire included the trombone, French horn, trumpet and tuba."[11] Music was a well-respected and practiced art in Greece and Rome. The person who had knowledge of music was regarded as a cultured person. During the Roman Empire, which includes the first two centuries of the Christian era, music played just as an important part of culture as architecture, philosophy, and new religious rites did. During the Roman Empire, popular virtuosos were brought in

8. Ibid., 7–8.
9. Ibid., 7–8.
10. Ibid., 23.
11. K Marie Stolba, *The Development of Western Music; A History,* 2nd ed. (Madison: Brown & Benchmark, 1994), 17.

from the Hellenistic world and performances and festivities were organized with large choruses and competitions. Many of the emperors were patrons of music, among them "Nero even aspired to personal fame as a musician."[12] Musicians often enjoyed privilege and status in this society.

Having basic knowledge of ancient Greek and Roman music is helpful in order to better understand the church's strong reactions to secular influence on sacred music.

Music with its styles, festivities, rhythms and modes made its way from Greece and the mixed Oriental-Hellenistic societies into the newly organized Christian Church. The Church tried to control the use of music. As step one, the church rejected certain aspects of ancient musical life. The church did not allow the cultivation of music purely for enjoyment as an art. Tied in with enjoyment as an art, the church rejected "the forms and types of music connected with the great public spectacles such as festivals, competitions, and dramatic performances, as well as the music of more intimate convivial occasions, not so much from any dislike of music itself as from the need to wean the increasing numbers of converts away from everything associated with their pagan past. This attitude even led at first to a distrust of all instrumental music."[13]

At first, it was believed that Christians imitated the worship services of the Jewish synagogue, but scholars today agree that early Christians actually avoided imitating Jewish services. They have done so to draw attention to the distinct character of their beliefs and rituals. However, one similarity was the singing of Psalms during the eve of Passover. Further investigation reveals the parallels that exist between the Temple sacrifice and the Christian Mass. As the Christian Church began to spread from Jerusalem through Asia Minor and into Europe and Africa, diverse musical elements from those regions began to make their way into the Church. For example, the churches and monasteries in Syria developed psalm singing and hymn singing. This practice made its way from Syria through Byzantium to Milan. It is here where the earliest hymn

12. Grout and Palisca, *A History of Western Music*, 23.
13. Ibid., 24.

singing is founded in the year 112 A.D. thus leading to the strophic type of singing called *kontakion*, or poetic elaboration on a biblical text. Rome became the central authority in musical development. It was here that the Western Church was increasingly Romanized. When Rome falls and Western Europe is born, musical influences develop in diverse places and cultures such as the Lombards, Franks, Goths and so on. However, the commonly used name for this strophic style of music is *chant*, which is defined as "music which is sung in accordance with prescribed ritual or tradition; in particular, the unaccompanied vocal music used for the services of the Christian church, in the Anglican church used only of the music to which the psalms and canticles are sung."[14] Since Rome is the center for music development, Western Music is linked with the music of the Roman Catholic Church.

Gregory the Great who was born around 540 CE and served as pope from 589 to 604 was a very influential pope not only in Rome, but also in Great Britain and surrounding countries. He successfully reformed Roman authority, worked in international and local politics, developed a welfare system, tax system, law and faith. Gregory was in favor of conformity in styles of worship. "The differing Latin liturgies (Mozarabic, Gallican, Ambrosian, Celtic) were gradually absorbed into the Roman Church, with an inevitable effect on the melodies that characterized them."[15] Since music was not written down during his time, musicologists have had a difficult time pinpointing the exact changes Gregory made to the liturgical structure, but nonetheless, he is the one credited with the changes made to the Roman liturgy. Gregory's influence was so significant that eventually the chants referenced above became known as Gregorian chants.

"Not only was the church vital in preserving music through the so-called Dark Ages, it was the center of activity of the community. The music of the church was an integral part of lay life; chants of the church were sung outside its walls and frequently served as

---

14. Westrup and Harrison, *The New College Encyclopedia of Music*, 114.

15. Andrew Wilson-Dickson, *The Story of Christian Music: From Gregorian Chant to Black Gospel* (Minneapolis: Fortress Press, 2003), 32.

the basis for secular songs."[16] Although, ecclesiastical chants were monophonic and without instrumental accompaniment, in light of music's growing popularity in the church, the Roman Catholic Church developed the order of Mass, a "setting of the Ordinary,"[17] This Mass contained five major parts, (1) *Kyrie eleison, Christe eleison*, Lord have mercy, Christ have mercy, (2) *Gloria in excelsis Deo*, Glory be to God on high, (3) *Credo in unum Deum*, I believe in one God, (4) *Sanctus, Sanctus, Sanctus*, Holy, Holy, Holy, and (5) *Agnus Dei, qui tollis peccata mundi: miserere nobis*, Lamb of God, who takest away the sins of the world; have mercy on us. This Mass is an example of a shift in church music from being simplistic to becoming more compositionally complex.

Composers began to improvise on these basic five components of the Mass and introduced other melodic lines, melisma and variations. A woman by the name of Hildegard of Bingen founded the convent in Rupertsberg, Germany. She wrote not only music for the Mass, but in 1151 wrote a musical play, *Ordo virtutum*, The Virtues, for entertaining purposes only. Around 1100 music began to evolve from one melodic line of chant to a new form called *organum*, "a method of composition used in the several stages of medieval polyphony"[18] where the melodic line was sung by the majority of singers and fewer singers would sing mostly note-against-note above the chant. From organum, the composition of polyphonous was increasing where a second voice either harmonized the chant above or below range or held longer notes while the melodic line continued. As harmonic progressions began to develop, composers were ready to expand the choral range as well. There was a move from writing chants with one melodic line to writing motets for two parts and three parts. In this earlier development of music, when instruments were used to play along with singers, they only played what the singers sung. In other words, the instruments did not accompany the singers, but played along with them. Eventually, this would change too.

16. Stolba, *The Development of Western Music*, 31.
17. Westrup and Harrison, *The New College Encyclopedia of Music*, 345.
18. Ibid., 398.

Reacting to New Music

Guillaume de Machaut, canon of Rheims and of St Quentin, spent much of his time writing poetry and music. "In spite of his holy orders and with a few notable exceptions, his creative energies were devoted to writing long, elegant and sophisticated love-poems, some of which he set to music. Some of the love-lyrics he wrote in his sixties were inspired by his relationship with a nineteen-year old girl."[19] His rebellion towards the church began when he started to blend secular themes with sacred.

As music develops into the Renaissance period, the church not only feels threatened by new styles of music coming from composers, but also the religious reformers opposed to the Roman Catholic Church. However, before the reformers are introduced into the picture, we will look at how the church reacted to inventions of a contemporary composer named Claudio Giovanni Antonio Monteverdi.

Monteverdi was born in Cremona in 1567 to a doctor. His musical talents earned him a job as violist in service to the Duke of Mantua. Later, in 1612, he became *maestro di cappella*, chapel master at St. Mark Church in Venice. In 1632, Monteverdi was ordained as priest. He wrote many compositions for church and for secular entertainment purposes as well. In the meantime, the invention of instruments also evolved and bowed instruments appeared such as the violin and viola de gamba. Somewhere around 1638, Monteverdi invented a new technique of playing for string instruments. He called this new technique, *pizzicato*, plucked. Monteverdi instructed the players to pluck the string with two fingers from the right hand while they hold on to the bow. When this technique was introduced in church, condemnation was proclaimed upon Monteverdi as being devil possessed and his inspirations coming from evil angels. This condemnation did not stop the great composer and inventor from continuing to explore the possibility of his instruments and inventing another new technique, this time, for bowed instruments called *tremolo*, "the quick and continuous reiteration of a single pitch. It is produced by a rapid

---

19. Dickson, *The Story of Christian Music*, 54.

up-and-down movement of the bow."[20] When this new technique was introduced in church, Monteverdi was literally pulled out of the church and condemned of being the devil himself. Needless to say, the church did not seem willing to accept anything new from these composers.

Composers were not the only threat to church music. The reformers across Europe were also posing a threat to the conservative Roman Catholic Church. Andrew Wilson-Dickson commented about John Wycliffe, "it seems surprising that he died in his own parish of Lutterworth in Leicestershire with his head still on his shoulders (in 1384)."[21] Wycliffe was an Oxford scholar and theologian who boldly attacked and condemned the sale of indulgences and the doctrine of transubstantiation. As he boldly believed people ought to read the Bible in their own language, he translated the Bible into English, but also sought to reform music in its worship format. He described the church music of his time with very strong language.

> "In the old days, men sang songs of mourning when they were in prison, in order to teach the Gospel, to put away idleness, and to be occupied in a useful way for the time. But those songs and ours do not agree, for ours invite jollity and pride, and theirs lead to mourning and to dwelling longer on God's Law. A short time later vain tricks began to be employed – discant, contre notes, organum and boquestus . . . which stimulate vain men more to dancing than to mourning . . . When there are forty or fifty in a choir [sic!], three or four proud and lecherous rascals perform the most devout service with flourishes so that no one can hear the words, and all the others are dumb and watch them like fools."[22]

The Roman Catholic Church needed to make a decision about how to handle Wycliffe's writings that encouraged the

20. Don Michael Randel, *The New Harvard Dictionary of Music* (Cambridge: The Belknap Press of Harvard University Press, 1986), 868.

21. Dickson, *The Story of Christian Music*, 55.

22. John Wycliffe, *Sermon on the Feigned Contemplative Life* (London: Hope Pub Co, 1967), 105.

transformation of worship, doctrine, music and liturgy. A series of harsh and severe actions followed against Wycliffe. Although he died of natural causes on December 30, 1384, he was still declared a heretic years after his death on May 4, 1415 at the Council of Constance. According to historian John Foxe, forty-four years after Wycliffe's death, in 1428, Pope Martin V gave the order to have Wycliffe's corpse exhumed and burn it. His ashes were thrown into the River Swift. Clearly, the church was intent on sending a message to other potential offenders.

Dickson called the theological Reformation process taking place in the Renaissance, but when it came to music, liturgy and worship, he referred to it as "a rebirth which challenged and undermined the cosmology of the Middle Ages . . . The church, its music and liturgy, was on the brink of profound transformation."[23] Changes, transformation, and rebirth were taking place simultaneously in different parts of Europe. Wycliffe began his rebellious transformation in England. Then, Jan Hus, inspired by Wycliffe's writings, began reformation in Bohemia; Erasmus Roterodamus in Rotterdam; and Martin Luther in Germany. Others would follow much to the church's displeasure.

The invention of the printing press by Johannes Gutenberg around 1438 was to the church's disadvantage during this controversy. The printing press aided in the growing ease of the dissemination of new music and new techniques for instrumentalists. The new hymnals by Martin Luther were printed at an alarming rate and spread all over Germany within a very short period of time. Although Luther was very familiar with the traditional Gregorian chant, he composed mostly in the polyphonic style of the time. According to Dickson, "in common with the ancient Greeks, [Luther] knew the power of music, for good and ill."[24] Concerning the power of music, Luther himself wrote, "Next to the Word of God, music deserves the highest praise. She is a mistress and governess of those human emotions . . . which control men or more often overwhelm them . . . Whether you wish to comfort the

23. Dickson, *The Story of Christian Music*, 58.
24. Ibid., 60.

sad, to subdue frivolity, to encourage the despairing, to humble the proud, to calm the passionate, or to appease those full of hate ... what more effective means than music could you find?"[25] Luther affirmed the same beliefs of music's power to influence and even shape people. However, Luther was compelled to use this power for God's kingdom instead of shunning it like other leaders in the church. Although, he received strong criticism from the Roman Catholic Church, Luther encouraged people to sing and to embrace sacred music that had become so controversial.

> "That singing hymns is good and acceptable to God is, I think, known to every Christian; for everyone is aware not only of the example of the prophets and kings in the Old Testament who praised God with song and sound, with poetry and psaltery, but also of the common and ancient custom of the Christian church to sing Psalms. St. Paul himself instituted this in I Corinthians 14 and exhorted the Colossians to sing spiritual songs and Psalms heartily unto the Lord, so that God's Word and Christian doctrine might be instilled and implanted in many ways.
> Therefore I, too, in order to make a start and to give an incentive to those who can do better, have with the help of others compiled several hymns, so that the holy Gospel which now by the grace of God has risen anew may be noised and spread abroad."[26]

Thus, Martin Luther himself is a champion of using music within the church to praise God, spread the Gospel, and as an evangelistic tool to be used in other countries. He not only encouraged, but also wrote and compiled several hymns for that purpose. The hymns of Luther were so influential that the "German Jesuit Adam Contzen lamented in 1620 that – from the Jesuit point of view – Martin Luther had destroyed more souls with his

---

25. Friedrich Blume, *Protestant Church Music* (London: Victor Gollancz, 1975), 10.

26. Martin Luther, *Geystliche Gesangk Buchleyn* (Wittenberg, 1524), LW53:315–316.

hymns than with all his writing and preaching."²⁷ Martin Luther printed the Wittenberg Hymnal that caused much controversy in Germany.

Robert Scribner believes that music during the time of Reformation was nothing more than a prominent means for propagating Reformation ideas. Christopher B. Brown states, "Lutheran hymns proved an effective means of spreading Evangelical ideas."²⁸ Brown continues to make a very important statement that fits in perfect harmony with the music ministry I seek to develop, "many of the early Lutheran hymn melodies sound far more like dance tunes than dirges, with their leaps and syncopated rhythms – features that already in Bach's time had begun to be suppressed. Though there is scant truth to the canard that Luther adopted the melodies of the tavern for his hymns."²⁹ Although, this music was up for debate, the comment by Christopher Brown that Lutheran hymns proved effective in reaching people was evidence to the reformers that God was moving through this music.

John and Charles Wesley worked together in writing new hymns. John often edited the hymns Charles wrote and even corrected its theological mistakes. For example, Charles wrote a hymn entitled, *Written for Midnight*. Before publication, it was given to John for editing who noticed one of the lines stated, *Since Death alone confirms me His*. John wrote a "big emphatic 'NO!'" on Charles' manuscript."³⁰ The hymns and poetry Charles Wesley had written were personal experiences and struggles he felt during his ministry. For example, Charles has published a hymn under the title *An Hymn for Seriousness* in the work *Hymns and Sacred Poems* that shares his spiritual state during his Georgia ministry. John R. Tyson suggests that this poem was to be autobiographical.³¹

---

27. Christopher Boyd Brown, *Singing the Gospel; Lutheran Hymns and the Success of the Reformation* (Cambridge: Harvard University Press, 2005), 1.

28. Ibid., 9.

29. Ibid., 19.

30. John R. Tyson, *Assist Me to Proclaim; The Life and Hymns of Charles Wesley* (Grand Rapids: William B. Eerdmans Publishing Company, 2007), 26.

31. Ibid., 34.

Charles continued to write songs based on his experiences, such as the hymn he wrote on May 23, 1738 that was for his evangelical conversion celebration.[32] After he was called to be an evangelist in 1738, his musical compositions began to serve as an evangelistic tool for the early Methodists. Tyson recorded about the later works of Charles, "His open-air, spontaneous evangelism and his gospel hymns were married together to form an effective tool for challenging people to live holy lives."[33]

As music in Europe was evolving, despite the Roman Catholic Church's effort to remain faithful to traditional music, music in Africa was also taking shape towards a different direction. While European music emphasized a balanced importance between melody, harmony, rhythm, instrumentation and lyrics, African music seemed more emotionally charged with an emphasis on rhythm as it pertained to the overall feeling being conveyed. African rhythm was more complex than European rhythm. While European rhythm focused on one simple rhythm at a time per musical piece, African rhythms overlapped each other in as much as two, three or four rhythms simultaneously while instrumentation was very basic or next to nothing. The melodic line was also very basic, if there was any at all, and African traditional music embraced the belting of words instead of the more reserved European style of singing.

---

32. Ibid., 48.
33. Ibid., 71.

5

A New Style is Born
The Amalgamation of European Music with African Music in the USA

IN THE UNITED STATES, these two styles of music have met and a process of amalgamation has begun. European music was brought over by settlers fleeing religious persecution in Europe while African music was brought over by slaves.[1] The amalgamation began in New Orleans. New Orleans music history and traditions including Jazz, funeral dirges, gospel brunch, and Congo Square are some examples.[2] "The fact is, many of the distinctive practices and experiences that inform the black church and its worship today have been passed on from generation to generation by the spiritual ancestors who were brought on the Middle Passage from Africa."[3]

---

1. "How the Slave Trade Affected Music: an Introduction," Sound Junction, accessed on October 3, 2013, http://www.soundjunction.org/howtheslavetradeaffectedmusicanintroduction.aspa.

2. "Music History," NewOrleansOnline, http://www.neworleansonline.com/neworleans/music/musichistory (accessed 3 October 2013).

3. Pedrito U. Maynard-Reid, *Diverse Worship: African-American, Caribbean & Hispanic Perspectives* (Downers Grove: Inter Varsity Press, 2000), 4.

African slaves in the new world used music not only as a tool of evangelism to keep their faith and heritage strong, but also, as it became, a deeper a part of life. In his book, Peter Randolph describes a "hush harbor":

> "Not being allowed to hold meetings on the plantation, the slaves assemble in the swamps, out of reach of the patrols. They have an understanding among themselves as to the time and place of getting together. This is often done by the first one arriving breaking boughs from the trees and bending them in the direction of the selected spot. Arrangements are then made for conducting the exercises. They first ask each other how they feel, the state of minds, etc. The male members then select a certain space, in separate groups, for their division of the meeting. Preaching in order, by the brethren; then praying and *singing all around,* [italics applied] until they generally feel quite happy."[4]

These hush harbors were a safe haven and a creative space for the slaves to develop a sense of faith in their own community. The feelings that were generated here must have been very powerful, and it was not coincidental that singing was a significant component to this communal gathering of uplift, worship and exhortation.

Classical composers such as George Gershwin, Aaron Copland, John Adams, John Cage, Samuel Barber, and others experimented with African syncopation and augmented chords that eventually lead to certain Big Band and Jazz styles. The size of the orchestra shrunk immensely form the large European Symphony Orchestra. On the other hand, percussion dominated songs began to evolve with just one instrument playing the bass, another playing chords and perhaps one saxophone filling in while the singer sung a very basic and limited melodic line. The drum set did not play the complex African rhythm, but it did shift accent from the natural beat of the Universe of one and three to off beats two and four. This over emphasized rhythm in offbeat pattern, made way

---

4. Ibid., 54.

A New Style is Born

for music to go into a completely different direction where its subconscious power could be used to hypnotize listeners.

In the past, Philosophers were aware of the power music has as mentioned earlier. If music has healing power, as Saul knew when he hired David to play his lyre for him, it must be concluded that it also has decaying powers. Musicologists, Donald Grout, Andrew Wilson-Dickson and K Marie Stolba, music therapists, Dr. Jen Klich in particular, and theologians, Louis Torres and Samuele Bacchiocci, have further explored the effect of music upon the human body and mind in the 20th century. One huge turn that causes much danger and decay in the new style of Rock-n-Roll is the technique of *backmasking*.

"Backmasking is a recording technique in which a sound or message is recorded backward on to a track that is meant to be played forward. Backmasking is a deliberate process, whereas a message found through phonetic reversal may be unintentional. The Beatles, who used backward instrumentation on their 1966 album, Revolver, popularized Backmasking. Back masking has become a tool to use in order to have music serve as an evangelistic tool. The new music style is geared to target young people, especially teenagers. Artists have since used backmasking for artistic, comedic and satiric effect, on both analogue and digital recordings. The technique has also been used to censor words or phrases for "clean" releases of explicit songs."[5]

Although David over and over called his people to praise the Lord and bless His name through music by singing and/or playing musical instruments, in the 1950s musicians changed course from praising God or singing about nature and love songs to worshipping Satan. "The backwards playing of records was advised as training for magicians by occultist Aleister Crowley, who suggested in his 1913 book that an adept "train himself to think backwards by external means," one of which was to "listen to phonograph records, reversed."[6] It created chaos in the American

---

5. Mark Sullivan, "'More Popular Than Jesus': The Beatles and the Religious Far Right," *Popular Music*, vol. 6, no. 3 (1987): 313–326.

6. Aleister Crowley, *Magick in Theory and Practice* (Newburyport: Red

families as more and more young people were drawn to this new type of music without knowing or realizing its dangers. The term itself, *rock-n-roll*, according to Morgan Wright, "was originally a nautical term which has been used by sailors for centuries. It refers to the rock (fore and aft motion) and roll (sideways motion) of a ship. The expression can be found in English literature going back to the 1600's, always referring to boats and ships. The term entered black spiritual music in the 1800's: "Rockin' and Rolling in the arms of Moses."[7]

Now, here is the origin of rock and roll music as we know it today. Before 1947, the main body of music that uses the term "rocking" is Negro Spirituals. Some song titles are "Rock my soul in the bosom of Abraham," "Rock me Jesus," "Rock me in the cradle of Thy love," "Rock me Lord," and "Rock Daniel," which date back to the late 19th century. "Rocking" was a term used by African Americans for the rapture they experienced at certain religious events, and the term also referred to the powerful rhythm found in the music that accompanied that religious experience. At the same time, black secular musicians were using the term for either dancing or sex, or both."[8]

Musicians knew of its effect and power because they used it in order to avoid punishments, fines and/or sanctions. Geraldo Rivera began a TV talk show in 1987 under his first name *Geraldo*. During the course of one episode, Geraldo investigated a very sensitive topic where priests from the satanic church were invited to talk about the connection of satanic worship, heavy metal and teenage suicide. The show was entitled, *Devil Worship: Exposing Satan's Underground*. It aired on October 22, 1988.[9] Geraldo was trying to prove some music groups like Metallica, Black Sabbath,

---

Wheel/Weiser, 1913), 64.

7. http://www.hoyhoy.com/dawn_of_rock.htm (accessed 17 February 2014).

8. "Dawn of Rock," HoyHoy.com, accessed on February 17, 2014, http://hoyhoy.com/dawn_of_rock.htm (accessed 17 February 2014).

9. "The Geraldo Rivera Show Devil Worship: Exposing Satan's Underground," http://www.imdb.com/title/tt1136645 (accessed 3 October 2013).

A New Style is Born

Slayer, Judas Priest, Motley Crue, KISS, Led Zeppelin, and others were openly professing to be Satan worshippers and/or performing satanic rituals before their concerts. Those rituals included but were not limited to drinking blood, shooting up cocaine, and wearing the pentagram pointing down instead of up with or without a goat head in it. One example is Ozzy Osbourne, who openly professed to be a Satan worshipper. Another was Jimmy Page, lead guitarist of the group Led Zeppelin who lived in the house of the late Aleister Crowley.[10] Aleister Crowley was a British philosopher and occultist. He was a ceremonial occultist, practiced black magic, and was responsible for founding the religion of Thelema.[11] While Jimmy Page lived in Crowley's old house he tried to contact the dead through rituals described by Crowley and also performed satanic rituals in his basement. This pointed to the negative impact of music and would support the church's position not to mix the secular with the sacred. While Geraldo may be correct in stating that those Rock and Heavy Metal group musicians were Satan worshippers and several teenagers listening to their music committed suicide, the link to connect the two is not complete. For example, Geraldo failed to examine the family situation at home of those teenagers. Some of the questions Geraldo should have asked, *Did those teenagers that committed suicide have a good relationship with their parents? Did those teenagers come from a broken home? Were those teenagers in problem with the law? What did their social life look like at school? Were they victims of bullying? Etc.* It is not my intent to defend and promote the Rock and Heavy Metal groups that these teenagers listened to prior to committing suicide, but simply want to make the point that it is possible that these teenagers were at the brink of harming themselves without listening to music. It is possible that music was the last straw that pushed them overboard.

10. "The 10 Wildest Led Zeppelin Legends, Fact-Checked," Rolling Stone, http://www.rollingstone.com/music/lists/the-10-wildest-led-zeppelin-legends-fact-checked-20121121/jimmy-page-once-owned-aleister-crowleys-former-home-19691231 (accessed 3 October 2013).

11. Aleister Crowley, *The Confessions of Aleister Crowly: An Autohagiography* (New York: Arkana, 1989), X.

Crowley's philosophy and drug addictions influenced other singers and groups in the rock-n-roll and heavy metal industry. "The Beatles included him as one of the many figures on the cover sleeve of their 1967 album *Sgt. Pepper's Lonely Hearts Club Band*, where he is situated between Sri Yukteswar Giri and Mae West. Jimmy Page was more intently interested in Crowley. Despite not describing himself as a Thelemite, Page was still fascinated by Crowley, and owned some of his clothing, manuscripts and ritual objects. During the 1970s, Page bought Boleskine House, which appeared in the band's movie *The Song Remains the Same*.

On the back cover of the Doors album entitled *13*, Jim Morrison and the other members of the Doors are shown posing with a bust of Aleister Crowley. Heavy metal musician Ozzy Osbourne released a song titled *Mr. Crowley* on his solo album *Blizzard of Ozz*, while a comparison of Crowley and Osbourne in the context of their media portrayals can be found in the *Journal of Religion and Popular Culture*.[12]

The music industry took a different turn when such musicians began talking about their concerts as worshipping the devil or welcomed their audience to Satan's sanctuary, as they called it. Within only about twenty years of music evolvement, it changed so much that the groups did not have to use back masking to get their messages across, they were allowed to share their satanic messages openly. Below is a sample from the repertoire of a heavy metal band called *Motorhead*. One of their songs entitled *Don't Need Religion*,[13] was recorded in 1992.

This rebellious type of music under rock-n-roll has brought about changes in the Christian arena as well. According to Robert S. Ellwood, Jr., "Young people in considerable numbers [are] rejecting both conventional Christianity and 'counter culture' religions to take up with evangelical Christianity. Incense and soft

---

12. Gary Crowley, *Band Explosion*, (1991), retrieved on June 19, 2011.

13. "Don't Need Religion," Motorhead, accessed on October 3, 2013, http://www.sing365.com/music/lyrics.nsf/Don't-Need-Religion-lyrics-Motorhead/D04Cd4168806725948256C55000C55DF (accessed on 3 October 2013).

chants to Krishna or Buddha [give] place to the sawdust and joyous hallelujahs of frontier-type camp meetings."[14]

Arthur Blessitt, "at the age of seven, he accepted Christ at a revival meeting. In the late 1960s Blessitt began evangelizing to the youth of Hollywood, California. There he became known as the 'Minister of Sunset Strip.' Blessitt preached to hippies, Hells Angels, runaways, drug addicts, teen prostitutes, flower children, would-be actors, and rock stars. In March 1968, he opened a coffee house called *His Place* in a rented building next door to a topless go-go club. It was there that he first made a big cross to hang on the wall of the building on the inside. He started carrying the cross on Sunset Strip from time to time."[15] According to Blessitt, there were at least 500,000 runaways annually during the late 60s and 70s. During the same years, "church attendance in the U.S. fell from 49% to 40% . . . the press talked of drugs, eastern religions, and the "death of God."[16] Although the Jesus movement was enthusiastically reaching out to hippies, drug addicts, eastern religion converts, the number of converts back to organized religion "was less than one half of 1 percent of the U.S. population and would not be enough to modify the declining church attendance figure of 1 percent a year."[17] As young people were drawn to rock concerts where they experienced sexual adventures, drug use, dancing and "trips" into Eastern religious experiments, Larry Norman played music with themes as *Jesus rock*, where he would try to "make a bridge from that world to the Jesus movement."[18] The Jesus movement was not an organized religious group or movement, but different denominations reacted in different ways to reach out to these run-aways, hippies, drug addicts, flower children, etc. For example, evangelical ministers would open a coffeehouse. One

---

14. Robert S. Ellwood, Jr., *One Way: The Jesus Movement and Its Meaning* (Englewood Cliffs: Prentice-Hall, Inc., 1973), ix.

15. "Life Lessons A-Z," Arthur Blessitt, http://www.blessitt.com/LifeLessions_A_Z/Master_Tab_Page1.html (accessed 17 February 2014).

16. Ellwood, *One Way*, 7.

17. Ibid., 8.

18. Ibid., 22.

was called *The Living Room* in San Francisco; a Congregational minister opened another one called *Bread and Wine*; and the *Salt Company Coffee House* was opened in Hollywood and supported by the Hollywood Presbyterian Church. At the Salt Company Coffee House, the "décor and music typical of the Salt Company is country-western rather than psychedelic and rock. Evenings at the coffeehouse present music with a Jesus slant combined with scripture and an evangelical appeal to listeners to declare their love for Christ made by a young, mod-dressed entertainer."[19]

According to Ellwood, "the great vehicle of the Jesus movement was music. The ability of Jesus rock and gospel melodies to generate rich, powerful feelings in a mood and emotion-oriented age has brought and held the movement together. It is largely music that has made the movement a part of pop culture, and it is the Jesus movement as pop culture that distinguishes it from what is going on in the churches."[20] A key figure in this Jesus movement in the late 60s and early 70s was Duane Pederson. Pederson founded the *Hollywood Free Paper*, a Christian paper that although was supposed to be underground, was distributed from coast to coast. Pederson was a former nightclub magician and Bible School dropout, but now a Christian, made a promise to God to enrich one million people by the end of 1971. He worked diligently by writing and circulating his paper in over 450,000 copies, holding outdoor evangelistic services and Christian rock concerts.[21] He used music as an evangelical tool.

Music was used as an evangelistic tool by secular rock and heavy metal groups to attract young people away from God, away from church and away from pure and moral laws. This project, as similar ministries during the Jesus movement, also uses music as an Evangelistic tool but to draw young people back to God, back to church, and back to a pure and moral lifestyle.

---

19. Ibid., 59.
20. Ibid., 64.
21. Lowell D. Streiker, *The Jesus Trip: Advent of the Jesus Freaks* (Nashville: Abingdon, 1971), 45.

A New Style is Born

D. Bruce Hindmarsh wrote the following in his essay about the Swissair Flight 111 that was en route from New York to Geneva on the evening of September 2, 1998. Something went wrong with the plane and it suddenly plummeted 2,400 meters into the Atlantic Ocean off the coast of Nova Scotia, killing all 229 people on board. Many people hurried to the little village of Peggy's Cove including the Coast Guard, police, emergency officers and family members of passengers on the plane. "An army chaplain went to the water's edge and offered to pray with the grieving family of a nineteen-year-old California student. He led them in prayer, and then the family started to sing a hymn in four-part harmony, followed by "Amazing Grace." The chaplain noticed that the scene transfixed all the rescue workers and onlookers. He added, "Things like that were going on all day – amazing grace in the middle of incredible sorrow."[22]

Edith L. Blumhofer is the author of an essay entitled, *Fanny Crosby, William Doane, and the Making of Gospel Hymns in the Late Nineteenth Century*. In this essay, she makes the point that Crosby and Doane use music as an evangelistic tool to shape a "community of believers around the texts printed in the hymnal."[23] In her conclusion, Blumhofer quotes Crosby and Doane about a contemporary observation: "There is no surer road to popularity than to become the author of a popular tune that can be sung in church, Sunday school and home."[24] There is much evidence that this statement holds true just by looking at the popularity of Christian music today within mainstream society and the newer categories of "Christian Rap," "Christian Rock," "Christian Hip Hop," "Christian Country," and so on. This positive power of music and its usefulness as an evangelical tool is also true in my local ministry context.

---

22. Mark A. Noll and Edith L. Blumhofer, *Sing Them Over Again to Me: Hymns and Hymnbooks in America* (Tuscaloosa: The University of Alabama Press, 2006), 3.

23. Ibid., 169.

24. Keith Watkins, "A Few Kind Words for Fanny Crosby," *Worship* 51, no. 3 (May 1977): 248–59.

Worship Music in the 21st Century

Music Ministry ought to make a difference in North America. It should be directed towards the needs of pre-teens and teenagers. They should be enlisted from the age of eight to the age of fourteen or when the student graduates from eighth grade. Once the student is enrolled in High School, he or she may come back as a volunteer to help young people go through the program. During the Music Ministry program children may come to receive tutoring help, sharpen their computer skills, do different activities, exercise physical education, and receive a free meal. In an open area students may get quiet reading time or play board games. The idea of Music Ministry for pre-teens and teenagers ought to be embraced in every inner city circle for underprivileged students. These are children that have no financial means to buy musical instruments or to pay for private lessons. Music lessons should be offered for free. Since it is a Christian faith based ministry, it must be open to prayer, mention the name of God freely, and teach Christian values and morals. Every lesson is geared towards helping students learn and develop musical skills by praising God for the gift of music and its positive power. Once the students accomplish learning to sing and play ten sacred songs, they will be invited to perform at Church in a concert format with their mentor. The impact of music on these students alone is a witness to the ability for God to use music to reach people in a transformative way no matter what controversy has been generated around it in the church. Although the results may not be seen immediately, the seed of the Gospel has been planted in their hearts and if not immediately, perhaps later in life that seed will spring up and bring fruits. As music will continue to be part of their lives and the instrument they have learned to play will continue to perhaps remain a hobby, the interest may spark again. The beauty of such a Music Ministry is that students are connected to music and God at the same time and that is the ultimate goal, to connect teenagers and pre-teens with God through the aesthetics of music.

6

Theological Aesthetics
How Human Beings are Drawn to God through Music

IT WAS MENTIONED SEVERAL times already that music is an art. It is a personal art unlike other art forms like sculpture or painting. When one looks at a sculpture or painting, the artist gives the abstract form, shape and colors. There is very little room for personal imagination or personal connection. With music however, it is different. I remember my first day in music history class. The professor asked us to close our eyes while he played several orchestral selections. When the piece ended, we were asked to open our eyes and share what went on in our imagination while listening to the musical selection. The result was fascinating. About fifteen students listened to the same music, but one imagined celestial bodies swirling, the other student imagined water falls, another student imagined a battle field and so on. Music is personal because it touches everyone on a personal level. Therefore, music could be a very powerful asset to use in Evangelism, but also to draw people into a closer relationship with Christ. Many churches use a lot of music and/or music concerts to make their revival weekend a success. It is important to realize that the revival is successful not because the band plays bad music that hijacks the senses, but because music touches everyone on a personal level. God may be approached through beauty, in this case, the beauty of music.

It is his beautiful character, beautiful creation, beautiful plan of salvation and the beauty of God allowing himself to be approached by his creations. It is through these aesthetics that the world may be reached for God. It is when one meditates on these theological aesthetics that he or she will truly realize the beauty and the artwork of the great master, God. This chapter will focus on analyzing the first two chapters of Genesis, which are regarded as God's Great Symphony of Creation, in order to examine God's beauty as it pertains to humanity.

Plato's idea that people experience certain things in the natural realm that are inherently true and good that transcend the natural, hence called transcendental, is a great launching pad for the premise that God may be approached through beauty. Indirectly, Plato identifies beauty as one of the transcendental. Plato argues that seeing forms and gaining knowledge about them is reaching beauty and knowledge of the beautiful. In this way, people are able to gain knowledge about God through manifestations of God's beauty in creation. Gesa Elsbeth Thiessen quotes Fyodor Dostoyevsky, a Russian essayist and philosopher, "with reference to Christ, that beauty will save the world."[1] The early church and leaders to the medieval times focused on the beauty of God, whether it is defined as visions of God or the purification of the physical eye or the eye of the soul since only a purified eye or eye of the soul may behold the beauty of God.

This concept of the beauty possessing a transcendent quality applies to the arts as well. Even though music is used primarily in worship, whether worshipping God or Baal, nature, love or beauty, history shows that the beauty of music has a transcendental quality. Art regarding the beauty of God has been a part of the church since the beginning. In the fourth century, there is a battle within the Roman Empire regarding pagan works of art. Bishops such as

---

1. Gesa Elsbeth Thiessen, *Theological Aesthetic: A Reader* (Grand Rapids: William B. Eerdmans Publishing Company, 2004), 5.

Theological Aesthetics

Gregory the Great "[commands] that all statues of Roman antiquity be thrown into the Tiber. Drowning them in the Tiber, instead of baptizing them into the church, [is] evidence that Christ had defeated Caesar."[2] Early leaders and bishops believe all pagan (secular) art must be destroyed for the sake of clean religion. For example, "seventh-century Pope Boniface [exhorts] him to destroy all idols 'under the sign of the cross', the image of a new construction of social reality."[3] According to Giorgio Vasari, "Christians [do] not do this 'out of hatred for the arts, but in order to humiliate and overthrow pagan gods. Nonetheless their tremendous zeal [is] responsible for inflicting severe damage on the practice of the arts, which then [fall] into total confusion."[4] Based on these incidents, people certainly believe that the arts have a quality to point beyond what is natural. In the instance of the dumping of pagan works of art into the Tiber, this points beyond the natural to an ideological reality that Caesar's empire has been brought down and that the Kingdom of Christ has been established. This line of reasoning is important as one considers God's beauty as it pertains to human experience.

A French Theologian and pastor during the Protestant Reformation, John Calvin, was strongly against the use of images, and presented challenges to the church surrounding the issue of sacred art. According to Calvin, no men could paint the God they had not seen because the human imagination is far more limited than the greatness and beauty of God. He wrote, "God has no similarity to those shapes by means of which people attempt to represent him . . . all attempts to depict him are an impudent affront . . . to his majesty and glory."[5] Calvin went as far as to call "the use of

---

2. John W. de Gruchy, *Christianity, Art and Transformation: Theological Aesthetics in the Struggle for Justice* (New York: Cambridge University Press, 2003), 11.

3. Venerable Bede, *The Ecclesiastical History of the English People* (Oxford: Oxford University Press, 1994), 88.

4. Gruchy, *Christianity, Art and Transformation*, 12.

5. John Calvin, *Institutes of the Christian Religion* II (Philadelphia: Westminster Press, 1960), 15–16.

images idolatry."[6] The point needs to be made that Calvin was not against art itself. He believed that secular art, whether painting or sculpture had its place in secular places where people did not worship. He wrote, "All arts, sculpture and painting amongst them, come from God and can bring pleasure."[7] However, he was against such art to be displayed in the sanctuary.

This confusion and struggle remained a constant thorn in Christianity's side until the nineteenth-century. Nietzsche, a critic of Christianity, insisted, "that Christianity has always been anti-aesthetic and antagonistic to art in principle."[8] Mary Charles Murry also addressed this issue in her thesis "that early Christianity was aniconic, the patristic evidence we have on art and Christianity was compiled by the Byzantine state in order to combat the use of icons in the church."[9]

However, some artists created their art as expression of their faith. One such artist was Rembrandt Harmenszoon van Rijn, a Dutch painter and etcher. He lived during the time of the most conservative Dutch Reformation period, the "most ultra-Calvinist of all reformed events, the Synod of Dort."[10] That did not stop Rembrandt from continuing to express his faith through his art, "went beyond it, leading it from earlier years of groping with the dichotomy of art and faith to the deeper understanding of art as an expression of faith."[11] According to John W. de Gruchy, "Christian theological aesthetics is, at its best, to ponder on the beauty that saves from the perspective of faith."[12] De Gruch goes a step further and makes the point that in order to see all that beauty of God in

---

6. Gruchy, *Christianity, Art and Transformation*, 41.
7. Calvin, *Institutes of the Christian Religion* II, 16.
8. Gruchy, *Christianity, Art and Transformation*, 17.
9. Ibid., 17.
10. Tim Gorringe, "Rembrandt's Religious Art," *Theology*, 98 (1995): 15f.
11. James R. Tanis, *Seeing Beyond the World: Visual Arts and the Calvinist Tradition* (Grand Rapids: Eerdmans, 1999), 16.
12. Gruchy, *Christianity, Art and Transformation*, 101.

art, one must be "brought within the orbit of Christian faith and made subject to Jesus Christ."[13]

Going back to music, it is an art form that always has the power to bring people and pre-teens into the unseen beauty of God. German Reformer, Martin Luther states, "That it is good and God pleasing to sing hymns is, I think, known to every Christian."[14] For missional purposes, Luther compiled a new hymnbook to spread the Gospel abroad. Luther bases his theology of singing on the words of Apostle Paul as he counsels the church in Corinth to sing about Jesus Christ and nothing else. In his preface to the Wittenberg Hymnal, Luther explains that he has arranged the new hymns into four-part harmony to please the young people, "to wean them away from love ballads and carnal songs and to teach them something of value in their place, thus combining the good with the pleasing, as is proper for youth."[15] Luther realizes the need to reach the youth and how the church must come up with ways to make the Gospel attractive to them. It is his desire to see art, especially music used by every pious Christian in the "service of Him who gave and made them."[16]

For example, according to David Bentley Hart, an Eastern Orthodox theologian, philosopher and cultural commentator, "the music of Bach is ultimate Christian music."[17] The musical composition process of Johann Sebastian Bach is of much importance to ministers today. Among his famous works are the Two-part Inventions. Bach's intention is to open the eye of the player to the possibilities of inventing new variations while staying true to the main theme. This process of generating new variations is of crucial importance to ministers as culture changes, while, at the same time, remaining faithful to the theologies of the church. According

---

13. Ibid., 102.

14. Paul Zeller Strodach, *Luther's Works: Liturgy and Hymns, Volume 53* (Philadelphia: Fortress Press, 1965), 315.

15. Ibid., 315.

16. Ibid., 316.

17. David Bentley Hart, *Beauty of the Infinite* (Michigan: William B. Eerdmans Publishing Company, 2004), 283.

to Bach, the possibilities of variations are endless as long as the pianist is creative. In his essay, *Created Beauty: The Witness of J.S. Bach,* Jeremy S. Begbie writes, "in sum, Bach seems far more intent on exploring the logic and potential of the musical material in hand than being driven by extramusical schemes of organization."[18] The beauty in Bach's music is the element of surprise. The listener cannot guess what will happen next, but all variations fit in perfectly with the original theme. This is the beauty of Bach's music. Although Bach lived during the Baroque period, his music is still admired and studied by jazz musicians in the twentieth-century for its improvisational qualities. Begbie is right when he writes that there is a "danger of thinking of beauty in terms of *closed harmonies,* about the particularizing, proliferating ministry of the Holy Spirit, effecting faithful but unpredictable improvisations on the harmony achieved in Jesus Christ."[19] The beauty and desire of Bach's music has survived for 300 years and it is just as fresh today as it was back when the great master played it himself.

Music has the power to promote its listeners into imagining and visioning the beauty of God. Music has the power to "help us perceive and understand that vision more deeply and clearly."[20] Bach was a faithful Lutheran and he intentionally composed to the glory of God. In 1747, three years before his death, Bach joined a "learned group, the corresponding Society of the Musical Sciences."[21] One of the members of this group wrote, "God is a harmonic being. All harmony originates from his wise order and organization . . . Where there is no conformity; there is also no order, no beauty, and no perfection. For beauty and perfection consist in the conformity of diversity."[22] According to Begbie, the

---

18. Jeremy S. Begbie, *The Beauty of God: Theology and the Arts,* ed. Daniel J. Treier, Mark Husbands and Roger Lundin (Illinois: InterVarsity Press, 2007), 36.

19. Ibid., 38.

20. Ibid., 39.

21. Ibid., 41.

22. Christoph Wolff, *Johann Sebastian Bach* (New York: W.W. Norton and Company, 2000), 466.

music of Bach not only provokes us to imagine, but also creates "a subtle relationship between natural and artistic beauty."[23]

Gesa Elsbeth Thiessen makes the point that later in time song and poetry writers have regarded song and poetry writing as art forms with the desire to capture the beauty of God's love. For example, Thiessen mentions poet George Herbert who gives titles such as *Church Musick* to his poems; Nikolaus Ludwig von Zinzendorf und Pottendorf who writes one of the best known Christian hymns, *Jesus thy blood and righteousness*; and Charles Wesley who, in his lifetime, writes a multitude of hymns, where the praise of Christ's marvelous love is captured.[24]

Today, art is just as important and vital to worship as it was in the early church. According to a three-volume set printed by the United Church of Christ, "it is an aid to worship and a means of theological and spiritual formation."[25] When this happens, de Gruchy argues, "art enables the church to fulfill its ministry in society."[26]

In the twentieth century, art takes a turn when artists shift to abstract and conceptual art. Music is affected by these developments as well. According to Thiessen, arts play an important role in theological aesthetics. Since church attendance is decreasing at an alarming rate, theology and arts are being addressed in different forums. "Scholars, sub-departments, research centers within faculties and conferences are [all] devoted to the theme."[27] For many of the educated middle class, especially in Europe, finding a museum or art gallery is their modern temple for spiritual nourishment and meditative experiences. Music is also being used as an art form to help people envision the beauty of God and experience the personal message of love that it brings.

---

23. Begbie, *The Beauty of God*, 43.

24. Thiessen, *Theological Aesthetic*, 157.

25. United Church Press, *Imaging the Word: An Arts and Lectionary Resource, Volume 2* (Cleveland: United Church Press, 1995), X.

26. Gruchy, *Christianity, Art and Transformation*, 213.

27. Thiessen, *Theological Aesthetic*, 205.

De Gruchy makes a very interesting connection between the Sanctuary and the Public Square. As the two are separated over the years by bishops, reformers and leaders by holding sacred art within the church building and secular art in the public square, "we need to keep firmly in mind that the church is not a building but a believing, worshipping and witnessing community of people. It is this community, both corporately and individually, which represents the church in the world. Nonetheless, church buildings also visibly represent what the church stands for physically and symbolically linking sanctuary and the public square."[28] Of course, today, it must be taken into account that some believers do not worship in traditional church buildings, but have house churches, storefront churches, mobile churches, warehouse converted churches, and so on. Often, this causes blurred lines between the sanctuary and the public square. This presents an interesting challenge as to distinguishing between the sacred and secular. However, it also presents new opportunities for God's beauty to be witnessed in new ways.

Music Ministry does not need to unfold in a traditionally recognized church building, but a former school building that has been converted into a non-profit ministry will suit the purpose just fine. Adolescents may worship God through the art of music and come in contact with the theological aesthetic of God through this experience. In D. Bruce Hindmarsh account of the Swissair Flight 111 that was en route from New York to Geneva on the evening of September 2, 1998, he witnesses many grieving families at the scene as one can imagine. Then, in the midst of bereavement, one family starts to sing *Amazing Grace* in four-part harmony. This turns into a corporate time of worship as other families join in and they start to sing more hymns together. In this moment of tragedy and despair, the beauty of God's love hovers over these families and becomes clear in the people's worship out by the water's edge. This does not happen in a church but it does not matter. The power of music transcends any limitations that location may seem to impose.

28. Gruchy, *Christianity, Art and Transformation*, 213.

De Gruchy makes the argument that "not all Christian art work [is] appropriate or acceptable in all Christian churches, or in all historical and cultural contexts, even though they are all dedicated to the worship of God revealed in Jesus Christ."[29] When cultural differences, ethnical practices or denominational rituals are taken into consideration, then the conclusion should be to respect the art that is uniquely distinct from one community to the next. Pie-Raymond Regamey makes the point that just because the artist is a non-believer or non-Christian it does not mean he or she cannot work for the church. A non-Christian artist may very well create a true sacred art because "a true artist is not a logician and it only requires a sacred character of the actual artistic creation."[30] Although the church's willingness to work with carefully selected non-Christian to produce sacred works of art could be an evangelical tool, this is not always perceived as beneficial arrangement with regard to preserving sacred trust.

According to the Vatican II Council, music is a very important art to be "preserved and cultivated with great care."[31] It was agreed that emphasis would be placed on the art of music by teaching music and musical activities in seminaries and every other gathering place in order for believers to learn to sing and play musical instruments to include them in the liturgical worship. Again, the power of music is recognized.

People, especially young people, are drawn to music that is easy to follow, pleasing to the ear, and catchy. In her essay *Fanny Crosby, William Doane, and the Making of Gospel Hymns in the Late Nineteenth Century*, Edith L. Blumhofer makes the point that Crosby and Doane use music as an evangelistic tool to shape a "community of believers around the texts printed in the hymnal."[32] In her conclusion, Blumhofer quotes Crosby and Doane about a

---

29. Gruchy, *Christianity, Art and Transformation*, 232.

30. Pie-Raymond Regamey, *Religious Art in the Twentieth Century* (New York: Herder and Herder, 1963), 190.

31. *Vatican Council II: Constitutions, Decrees, Declarations*, ed. Austin Flannery (New York: Costello Publishing Company, 1996), 152.

32. Noll and Blumhofer, *Sing Them Over Again to Me*, 169.

contemporary observation: "There is no surer road to popularity than to become the author of a popular tune that can be sung in church, Sunday school and home."[33] Blumhofer, Crosby and Doane are among many who understand the theological significance of sacred music.

John and Charles Wesley worked together in writing new hymns. John often edited the hymns Charles wrote and even corrected its theological mistakes. A common example of this was when John corrected Charles' hymn entitled *Written for Midnight*. Before publication it was given to John for editing who noticed one line in particular, "Since Death alone confirms me His." John wrote an emphatic "NO!" on Charles' manuscript.[34] In this regard, Wesley was wise. The way the line was written could send the message that Death is the key agent at work in sealing our relationship with God, which is grossly inaccurate from a Christian standpoint. Wesley could foresee this line creating confusion or misguiding people theologically so he had him change it before its publication.

Charles often wrote hymns based on personal experience and circumstance. On May 23, 1738, Charles wrote a conversion hymn that was sung the following night in "celebration of John Wesley's evangelical conversion."[35] According to Tyson, theologians debate about the actual hymn that was sung. Most theologians prefer *Where Shall My Wondering Soul Begin?* In 1738, ministry took a turn in Charles Wesley's life when he was called to become an evangelist. According to Tyson, Charles wrote a hymn regarding this new chapter in his life fifty years later. There was much turmoil during those fifty years. The people began to question the new beliefs, the Bishop of England began to question these new beliefs and practices, and, on June 19, 1739, Charles went to visit the Archbishop of Canterbury at Lambeth Palace. Through this experience, he wrote a hymn entitled, *Gamaliel's advice*. It became clear that his music took a turn as his ministry did. His music began to serve as an evangelistic tool for the early Methodists. Tyson

33. Watkins, *A Few Kind Words for Fanny Crosby*, 248–59.
34. Tyson, *Assist Me to Proclaim*, 26.
35. Ibid., 48.

recorded, "[Charles'] open-air, spontaneous evangelism and his gospel hymns were married together to form an effective tool for challenging people to live holy lives."[36] Charles Wesley was an excellent example for composers and performers today who sing about personal spiritual struggles and who use music as an evangelistic tool. People could relate to those personal struggles and would be inclined to join in such singing and praise. These hymns still resonate with people today.

At the Music Ministry program, students should be introduced to different styles and genres of music with varying instrumentations, melodic lines, harmonic progressions and rhythms to see which style is more appealing to their ears. Once the students choose the style that fits their culture according to their circumstance at home, it will be evident what lyrics and genres are attractive to them. The different styles include but are not limited to selections from the classical repertoire, Gospel, Jazz, Blues, Country, Bluegrass, Pop, and Rock-n-Roll. Different instrument choices should also be introduced to find out if students react better to natural classical instruments such as the violin, trumpet, and clarinet, or electric instruments such as the electric guitar, bass guitar, synthesizer and electric drums. The experiment should include a log to track the reaction of students to soft and natural rhythm of the classical repertoire or the louder and percussive rhythm of the drum set. Once these experiments have been conducted and the results are assessed, students may be taught and trained in the style and instrumentation of their preference with religious lyrics that are based on Christian values. Melodies could be borrowed from tavern tunes and rock songs just as Martin Luther and others have done, but the lyrics changed to teach Christian morals and values to introduce the students to God and God's divine loving character. The success of this project will be determined by the desire of the students to praise God, to continue being trained in the art of music, and their willingness to use their talents in church as worship leaders.

36. Ibid., 71.

According to Irenaeus, God has revealed himself through his prophets, but men "who bear his Spirit and always await his coming"[37] also reflect God's character. God needs men today who are willing to bear his Spirit and be witness for the Kingdom. When such men fulfill their calling, adults and children are drawn to the beauty of God through an aesthetics based approach to theology. According to Nicolas Berdyaev, "in Christian art there is always a transcendental intention towards another world, towards an upsurge beyond the limits of the immanent world; there is romantic longing . . . Christian art does not leave us in this world, in beauty already finally attained, but leads us out into another world, with beauty beyond and outside the limits of this."[38] Theological aesthetics, the art and beauty of God are "that ultimate, objective ground, the splendor or glory of God"[39] that children must see and experience.

This study shows that there should not be an issue with using contemporary instrumentation and musical styles with its rhythms and harmonic progressions for this project or for musical use in church. Borrowed melodies from taverns or other secular songs are also acceptable as an evangelical tool because these melodies tend to be well known, they are catchy to the ear and people enjoy singing them. Music from different parts of the world should be welcomed and accepted in their original form. The Vatican II Council has voted that "the art of our own times from every race and country should also be given free scope in the church, provided it bring to the task the reverence and honour due to the sacred buildings and rites."[40] The key is to permeate what is secular with the Gospel and not allow what is secular to contaminate the sacred.

Music had disappeared and was excluded from worship and church rites during the Reformation, but since has made its

37. Thiessen, *Theological Aesthetic*, 17.

38. Nicolas Berdyaev, *The Meaning of the Creative Act* (London: Victor Gollancz, 1955), 229.

39. Gruchy, *Christianity, Art and Transformation*, 103.

40. *Vatican Council*, 157.

way back into the church. Today, it is the dominant art form in Protestant and Charismatic traditions. John Dillenberger writes, "beyond the ordinary level in which music seems to please us, the structure of music may also affect, address, stretch, confirm, trouble the depths of our being in ways no other discipline does, not because it is better but because it represents a unique sensibility, analogous to but not identical with other sensibilities."[41] As different types of music prevail in the church today, it draws people to its message. For the church, music with words is more effective than just instrumental music since the words are what convey Christian theology. Dillenberger explains that music combined with language has intelligibility, and for Christians this ability to communicate artistically should point to Christ.

Thiessen offers an excellent concluding thought for the consideration of theological aesthetics. "Especially contemporary art, will not only play an increasingly important role in theology but hopefully it will gain and regain its place and importance in church life, i.e. in places of worship. In opposition to the many destructive images that surround us, art, like theology, may yet offer something different, something life-giving and life-affirming, a critical view of our existence, a call to change, a glimmer of hope, an anticipation of what may be and could be."[42] The Music Ministry project shares Jesus' burden to draw children to God and has found the art of music to be a useful evangelical tool in doing so. Music Ministries ought to be very excited about opportunities to use music for God's glory while simultaneously making disciples for Christ of the youngest members of our community.

---

41. John Dillenberger, *A Theology of Artistic Sensibilities: The Visual Arts and the Church* (London: Student Christian Movement, 1987), 247.

42. Thiessen, *Theological Aesthetic*, 249.

7

The Power of Music

Music Has the Power to Lead People to Conversion

As we have seen in previous chapters, music is a powerful art. It has the power to influence people to do something on a subconscious level as long as their pre-established principles allow. People may be influenced to do bad and harmful things, but they could be influenced to do good and constructive things to themselves, their families and their communities. That is why in some cultures music plays a huge part in their lives.

When Nelson Mandela was released from prison in South Africa in 1990 after a twenty-seven year prison term, all the supporters broke out in song and dance as they greeted their respected leader.[1] It was their way of celebrating Mandela's release. That day, over half a million people waited in the heat of the sun for him to appear in Cape Town. Those people also expressed their joy in song and dance. Mandela himself danced on his way to the podium.

---

1. Youtube Video, https://www.youtube.com/watch?v=s5H8bkdZy-Y; accessed March 3, 2015.

The Power of Music

In the small country of Estonia there is a tradition of Song Festival every five years where over 100,000 people gather to hear choirs as large as 15,000 in number. This song festival is called *Laulupidu*.[2] The birth of this song festival is an amazing story. Under the communist regime of Russia, the Estonians had very little to give them hope.

One of those little things they had was music, or to be more correct, singing. When Russia threatened them with war, violence and a deportation; a group of Estonians started singing their song on the streets. As they walked singing, more and more people joined in. By the time they reached the square in the capital, tens of thousands of people were singing. This is how the Estonians held off their Russian oppressors, by singing. Professor Rein Vandemann at the Tartu University said: "We had no fear while we were singing." Music has the power to give hope, courage and purpose with a direction in life. Many people in the US connect country music with way of life and express their feelings through music.[3] Toby Keith released a song, *I Love This Bar*, where all kinds people gather from all walks of life and nobody judges them based on dress, appearance or status. As I watched that song on YouTube, I began to wonder if my church ought to be a place like that. A place where all kinds of people may come regardless of how they look or what their past is like and they would be welcomed without judgment. After all, if the church is supposed to be a hospital for sinners and not a country club for saints, then why so many people find refuge at the local honky-tonk and not the church? I am afraid to quote Toby Keith's lyrics of the song here because of their graphic nature and the way Christians view that terminology. It seems as if the church would be afraid of reality and to speak of what is out there in real terms. Churches that stay away from such realities have little or no influence on their communities and little or no success rate in relating to people and relaying the good

2. Youtube Video, https://www.youtube.com/watch?v=Re1Lj3dHofc; accessed March 3, 2015.

3. Tex Sample, *White Soul; Country Music, the Church and Working Americans*, (Abingdon Press, Nashville, Tennessee, 1996).

news message of the Gospel. In such cases, music could play a very important role as icebreaker and bridge builder between church and community. Music can soften the heart, make emotional connections and even lead the soul to a religious conversion.

In this chapter we will look at how music has the power to lead one to conversion. As surprising as that may be, yes, music has the power to do that. Rob Vandeman, the executive secretary for the Columbia Union Conference of the Seventh-day Adventist Church, wrote in an article[4] about his new assignment as chairman of the board of Washington Adventist University's contemporary Christian radio station. Vandeman describes how this music is not his first choice to listen to, but about half a million listeners tune in to hear contemporary Christian music. According to Vandeman, this station is not about what we like, but "It is about the listeners and what God is doing in their lives." Music has the power to change lives, to change habits, to change thinking process, to change mentality, and to change the heart.

I have taught underprivileged children to play musical instruments and to develop their singing voices in order to become future music leaders in church. For that purpose not only their musical skills were being developed but their relationship with God also. As they grew in both the arts of music and spirituality, they were introduced to Jesus Christ as their personal Savior and invited into a closer walk with Him through conversion and commitment to serve using their new talents, in this case music.

We will look at the process of conversion, what it entails, what changes might be expected in the lives of the converts and what results it will bring forth. The Merriam Webster Dictionary defines the word *conversion* as a noun that is (1) "the act or process of changing from one form, state, etc., to another, (2) the act or process of changing from one religion, belief, political party, etc., to another."[5] "Religious conversion" is on the other hand

---

4. Rob Vandeman, *Music Can Change the World*, article for the Visitor magazine, (Pacific Press Publishing Association, Nampa, Idaho, February issue, 2015), 3.

5. http://www.merriam-webster.com/dictionary/conversion (accessed

described by Princeton.edu as "the adoption of a new religion that differs from the convert's previous religion."[6]

For a Music Ministry to be effective, one of the first questions to ask is the process of training and the methods used to accomplish that. What role will conversion play in the lives of students if they already do attend a church? How would their parents react to the idea of their child's conversion? The website mentioned earlier, Princeton.edu makes a distinction between *conversion* and *reaffiliation*. "Changing from one denomination to another within the same religion (e.g., Christian Baptist to Methodist, Muslim Shiite to Sunni, *etc*) is usually described as *reaffiliation* rather than *conversion*."[7] If some of the students are already attending a church and/or belong to a denomination with their parents, the challenge would become whether to proselytize the students into the new denomination by reaffiliation or (1) to invite them to serve as music leaders in a new denomination without a process of conversion, or (2) continue to train all students at the Music Ministry equally, but invite only those students to serve who are not affiliated with a church or denomination. Nonetheless, conversion is deeper than leaving one religion for another or joining one religion for a purpose or interest.

The French sociologist Daniele Hervieu-Leger specializes in sociology of religion, "observes that even as religious institutions are losing their regulatory power in society, conversion is on the increase. The author goes on to propose three types of conversion, including that from unbelief to religious belonging and belief, from one religious affiliation to another, and "reconversion" or a shift from nominal affiliation to lived practice and belonging within the same denomination."[8]

---

14 November 2013).

6. http://www.princeton.edu/~achaney/tmve/wiki100k/docs/Religious_conversion.html (accessed 14 November 2013).

7. Deirdre Meintel, *When There Is No Conversion: Spiritualists and Personal Religious Change*, Anthropologica, (Universite de Montreal, 2007, Canadian Anthropology Society), 49 (1): 149–162.

8. Daniele Hervieu-Leger, *Religion as a Chain of Memory*, (Rutgers University Press, New Brunswick, New Jersey, 2000).

According to the Fundamental Beliefs of the Seventh-day Adventist Church, "A spiritual development process is anticipated in the Christian life. Change for the Christian involves both conversion (John 3:3, 7; Acts 3:19; Rom 12:2; 2 Cor 5:17) and growth (Prov 4:18; Luke 2:52; Eph 3:17–19; 4:11–15; 2 Peter 3:18). At conversion, believers accept Christ's perfect life as their own by faith and experience a Spirit-led transformation of values (John 3:5; Gal 2:20). Both external and internal forces may provoke relapses in thought or conduct (Gal 5:16–18; 1 John 3:20), but commitment to grace-induced progress in the Christian life (1 Cor 15:10; Phil 3:12–14; Col 1:28, 29) and reliance upon God-provided resources (Rom 8:5–7; Gal 5:24, 25) will produce growth toward Christlikeness."[9] The Seventh-day Adventist Church believes the process of conversion ought to bring one closer to God in relationship and becoming Christ-like in word, thought, deed and daily life. Therefore it is not limited to mere believing, but also living it out in daily life.

A new idea within the church paradigm is to welcome people to sing, pray, study, praise God without forcing them into belonging. Meintel describes the Montreal Spiritualists as a group that has members who claim to be converted into their new religion but without the traditional rituals that are usually requested by other denominations. The most common practiced ritual of conversion and belonging is marked by the act of baptism. At the Harford Institute for Religion Research several scholars joined in to compile articles that was published as the *Encyclopedia of Religion and Society,* they agreed, "*conversion* in the religious literature, is a term with a more cognitive and emotional meaning and referring more to beliefs. Those who study social movements, including new religious movements, more often use terms such as *recruitment* , which has more of a behavioral connotation focused on participation."[10] This statement from the Hartford Institute for

---

9. *Seventh-day Adventist Fundamental Beliefs,* This statement was voted during the Annual Council of the General Conference Executive Committee on Sunday, September 27, 1998, in Iguacu Falls, Brazil.

10. Edited by William H. Swatos, Jr., *Encyclopedia of Religion and Society,*

THE POWER OF MUSIC

Religion Research resonates well with Music Ministry experiment because according to this definition conversion is more cognitive and emotional. A decision must be made to participate and use the musical talents learned to praise God in a house of worship and it ought to be emotional and personal. The personal emotional must be reflected in singing and/or playing a musical instrument as to draw the listeners into a closer relationship with God. The purpose is not only to train and have someone lead out the music part of worship, but to have someone who is passionate about God and is willing to express that passion through the art of music. This method of conversion excludes the practice of "brain washing," and "mind control." Praising God and leading out in music worship ought to be the individual's free choice built on personal love to God and music.

Sociologist Rodney Stark placed a new spin on the idea of conversion, "The research on joining the new religions was initially derived from literature in sociology and psychology of religion that shared a common assumption of something being wrong with a person who would seek religion is a "psychopathological" explanation of religious participation. The early literature in this psychopathological vein assumed that a person must be suffering some major deprivation or have had some major trauma in his or her life to be interested in religion—a "religion as crutch" perspective."[11] Carolyn Y. Johnson, staff of Boston Globe published an article in the paper January 3, 2013 under the title, "Is the person you are today the real, final you? Harvard study says you'll change more than you think."[12] This article exposes a Harvard study where the experiment proved that people will change over in the area of beliefs, ideas, and character. It is interesting to see Stark placing such a negative label on conversion. As much as

---

(AltaMira Press, A Division of Sage Publications, Inc., Blue Ridge Summit, PA, 1998).

11. Rodney Stark, *Becoming a World-Saver; American Sociological Review*, (Harper Collins and Princeton University Press, Princeton, NJ), 30–600.

12. Carolyn Y. Johnson, *Science in Mind; Is the Person you Are Today the Real, Final You? Harvard Study Says You'll Change More Than You Think*, (Boston Globe Newspaper, Printed on January 3, 2013).

there might be some people using religion as a crutch, it should not place all people in that same category. On the other hand if the church has a place for people who suffered major trauma in their lives, that church has reached the goal Jesus had in mind when He organized His 1st century church.

Another sociologist, Bainbridge, "uses the term *strain theories* to refer to such ideas within the sociological realm. This broad perspective also assumed a high degree of passivity on the part of the person being converted—he or she was defined almost as an object to be acted upon by external or internal forces—and the power to bring about a conversion was posited elsewhere than with the subject of the conversion/recruitment."[13] The idea of having an external or internal force acting upon the candidate is not in harmony with the privilege of freedom of choice each person must possess in regards to conversion. The only external force could be acceptable in leading a person to conversion is the Holy Spirit. But even the Holy Spirit allows room for freedom of choice.

Some denominations believe the process of conversion is also for the purpose of becoming recruiters for new converts. In his book Stark mentions a group called Moonies led by Miss Kim in the 1960s. Her group had very few converts in San Francisco during the 1960s, so she decided to pair them up by twos and send them out to different cities to recruit new converts. Some of those cities were Dallas, Denver, Berkeley and others. Within a short period of time the groups began to grow.[14] The purpose of a Music Ministry is not to train evangelists and recruiters, but to allow their love for God and music to speak for itself. If the attitude and success of students in the area of performance and leadership in music would draw others to accomplish the same, it would be their personal choice to join and participate.

13. William Sims Bainbridge, *The Sociology of Conversion; In Handbook of Religious Conversion,* Edited by H. Newton Maloney and Samuel Southard, (Religious Education Press, Birmingham, AL).

14. Rodney Stark, *The Rise of Christianity; How the Obscure, Marginal Jesus Movement Because the Dominant Religious Force In the Western World In a Few Centuries,* (Harper Collins and Princeton University Press, Princeton, NJ, 1996).

The Power of Music

In the same book, Stark makes an interesting comment about the role of women in church membership growth, "it should be noted that while secondary converts are often rather lukewarm about joining in the first place, once immersed in the group they often become very ardent."[15] The theology of this utopia is not to focus on recruiting new members constantly, but to spread the love of God and to help people find spiritual healing by participating in musical worship. If that should lead to conversion, the act of baptism, belonging and joining should not be denied.

In their book, Buckser and Glazier state, "Anthropologists have long argued that religion involves more than just ideas about the supernatural; it constitutes a theory of the world, a way of constructing reality that seems uniquely real to those who experience it. If this is true, how can it be that individuals suddenly choose new religions? To change one's religion is to change one's world, to voluntarily shift the basic presuppositions upon which both self and others are understood."[16] Such a conversion is not an easy change. The majority if not all ideas and theologies change, lifestyle changes and in most cases the circle of friends change as well. There must be solid foundation and reasoning for making such a change. If the conversion is limited to re-affiliation as described earlier, the change is not so extreme. Most theologies, doctrines, lifestyle and circle of friends remains the same or with very little change. One must have a very devoted desire to make such change in the process of conversion. Anthropologists Buckser and Glazier also make mention of the word *coercion* used by religious groups to recruit new converts. Coercion does not strike a cord with the project unfolding at Music Ministry for it is robbing the candidate of the privilege of freedom of choice.

According to the same anthropologists, conversion has a political dimension to it as well. A sincere convert will vote for a political leader that promises and fights to maintain religious freedom. Religion holds high moral standards for politicians.

15. Ibid.
16. Andrew Buckser and Stephen D. Glazier, *The Anthropology of Religious*, (Rowman and Littlefield Publishers, Inc., Lanham, MD 2003).

Music Ministry should not get involved in the political dimensions since the students participating may be too young to have political views or the privilege to vote. At this time, emphasis should be placed on learning music and getting to know God on a more personal level. Everything else is left to the discretion of the Holy Spirit.

Conversion is not an overnight experience. It is a life long process that ought to be experienced daily. Conversion involves a very deep and life changing decision that must entail study, prayer, meditation, time and patience. It is not the duty of the minister or instructor to decide when a person is ready for conversion, but it is the work of the Holy Spirit convicting the person. It is the duty of the minister, instructor, and teacher to make known what God offers and can do for those that accept those gifts. During the remainder of the conversion process the minister may assist in explaining God's Word or the calling of the Spirit, but the individual must make that life changing decision when ready, when attracted and when they have fallen in love with Jesus as their personal Savior.

If conversion is forced upon individuals or if they are coerced into it, it could very easily lead into a false conversion. False conversion causes harm and pain instead of joy and peace in serving God and fellow human beings. When false conversion occurs, the candidate may lash out to display disagreement, it may lash out to cause discord, or may lash out by abusing the talent to a far extreme. For example in the arena of music, instead of playing softly and in harmony with the other musicians, the coerced musician might play louder, more aggressively, might push the rhythm to a faster pace, or any other way that comes to mind just to create chaos. If conversion is forced upon individuals rather than allowing the Holy Spirit to work on their hearts and be drawn to Christ, those candidates will leave the church sooner or later with an angry heart towards the leadership and would continue to share their painful stories with people in their communities and circle of influence to prevent others from attending or considering to attend that particular church.

8

Arguments
People Trying to Defend or Attack Different Styles, Instrumentation, and Emotional Expressions

DURING MY TRAVELS IN different countries, different cultures and different surroundings, I was always fascinated with the selection of music that was used in worship. But I noticed more than just the selection of music, instrumentation, rhythm and melodic line, the manner in which it was performed. Some musicians stood still like some statues without any physical display of emotion while others smiled when happy songs of joy and praise was performed, and there were musicians that included body language into their performance. The body moved not in rhythm to give the beat, but it would move one direction for one phrase and another direction for the following phrase. All these musicians praised God by keeping their feet in the same spot throughout the song. Some even included hand gestures to emphasize the meaning of the song. There were also musicians that were completely free in their praise. They raised their head upward when they sang to God, raised their hands and for an added emphasis stomped their feet and shook their heads. And yes, there were musicians who could not stand still. They moved around by pacing back and forth, jumping up and down, and dancing before the Lord.

The congregations are usually divided regarding the freedom of musicians and parishioners during praise time. While some parishioners join in, others remain seated. Some parishioners raise their hands with their palms facing toward the heavens, while others only raise their hands just a little bit above their waistline. While some churches do permit the expression of joy through clapping, some congregations condemn it as a secular expression used in Baal worship. In this chapter we will look at some of the arguments people raise to defend or condemn these emotional expressions.

1. The musicians are not genuine; they just do it for the show

That may either be true or not be true. Who is the judge? When I was told this argument, I asked the person if he approached any of the musicians to ask them. The person did not ask any musician, only based his argument on personal interpretation. The Scripture is very clear on judging people, especially when there is no evidence to support it. This argument is only based on supposition. Jesus said in his Sermon on the Mount, "Judge not, that you be not judged. For with what judgment you judge, you will be judged; and with the measure you use, it will be measured back to you."[1] According to these words of Jesus, we are judged in the same manner as we judge others. Judgment based on supposition is very dangerous, and most of the time, false.

---

1. Matthew 7:1, 2 NKJV.

2. Musicians could express themselves in more limited body language. In other words, control themselves

It is always easier to fix others than self. Who is to decide what is acceptable and what is too far? Based on what should such decisions be made? David himself gives no limitations but simply says: Praise the Lord with shouting and dance.[2] The Bible verse that comes to mind is 1 Samuel 16:7, But the Lord said to Samuel, "Do not look on his appearance or on the height of his stature, because I have rejected him; for the Lord does not see as mortals see; they look on the outward appearance, but the Lord looks on the heart."[3] Again, this is a judgment based on supposition and outward appearance than the intention of the heart.

3. It is too loud/soft, slow/fast, boring/excitement, etc.

When these arguments are made, the church is divided on what type of music should be used for worship. This argument will be examined in more detail in the Conclusion chapter. However, in such contexts the parishioners are reluctant to look for a common ground where the selection of music would be acceptable to both sides and instead each is fighting for their own by condemning the other. Not only condemning each other, but take every argument to the extreme far away from the common ground as possible. I recommend that each group would look for songs, melodies, instrumentation, loudness volume and emotional expressions that are acceptable to both sides and learn to grow from there together. That means each side has to give and take a little. There is no competition here, it does not mean one side has to lose and the other has to win, but to learn to worship and praise God together. After all, we are heading towards the same Kingdom. Apostle Paul makes it clear that we are on the same team headed for the same reward, "Therefore you are inexcusable, O man, whoever you are who judge, for in whatever you judge another you condemn

2. See Psalms 149 and 150.
3. 1 Samuel 16:7 NRSV.

yourself; for you who judge practice the same things."[4] There was a rift among the Jews and the Gentiles regarding circumcision and other minor things. Paul simply wrote to them counseling them to practice as they feel in their hearts and stop judging those that see it otherwise.

4. New music is too crazy.

New was never the norm or the appreciated in history. Not only music, but all arts, including painting, sculpture, writing, fashion, etc. Those visionaries that led the innovation were not appreciated either, in some cases were cast out of the church as we have seen the story of composer Monteverdi. That is why many artists who were ahead of their times died either young or early death because of illness, poverty, malnutrition, etc. Their music and art is greatly appreciated today, but it was not appreciated when it was new. We could only speculate how many more great masterworks we would have today from Beethoven if he would have been appreciated during his lifetime, or how many more great masterworks we would have today from Mozart if he would have been appreciated during his lifetime, and so on? One solution is to keep an open mind, study about it, get as much information as possible on it and give it a try. It might work, or it might not. Most of the new art forms are rejected not because they are theologically or musicologically incorrect, but because some do not like it.

5. Christian Rock is bad because it is Rock music with sacred words

This question will also be dealt in greater detail in our Conclusion chapter, however this argument has no theological or musicological bases either. While it may be true that Christian Rock uses similar techniques, elements, instruments, rhythms and melodic shapes as Rock music, there is still a huge difference. In Christian

---

4. Romans 2:1 NKJV.

Rock, the lyrics do not sing about devil worship, incest, secular themes, but worships God. Is all Christian Rock good? No. Is all Christian Rock bad? No. There is a measuring rod that helps people make wise decisions regarding this genre. If it helps you connect with God, use it. If it does not help you connect with God, do not use it. Whether or not this helps you, do not judge those that are helped by it.

Should we discard it just because the origin is bad (this is questionable as well)? Let us look at two examples that have a really bad origin and yet we appreciate them today even in the Christian world. One example is Christmas. The entire Christian world celebrates Christmas as the birth of Christ on December 25. All theologians that have done extensive research on the birth of Christ come to the conclusion that Christ, the babe, was not born on December 25. Looking at the details given to us in the Gospel of Luke, Jesus' birthday cannot be in December. I will share some details here. The decree from Caesar Augusts to register all people was done in late summer, early fall. It would make it impossible for many people to walk long journeys to register in the middle of winter. Another detail is the description of the shepherds in the field. The sheep were out in the field. This again is impossible in the middle of winter. For more details you may research the works of Dionysius Exiguus. "Joseph A. Fitzmyer – Professor Emeritus of Biblical Studies at the Catholic University of America, member of the Pontifical Biblical Commission, and former president of the Catholic Biblical Association – writing in the Catholic Church's official commentary on the New Testament, writes about the date of Jesus' birth, "Though the year [of Jesus birth is not reckoned with certainty, the birth did not occur in AD 1. The Christian era, supposed to have its starting point in the year of Jesus birth, is based on a miscalculation introduced ca. 533 by Dionysius Exiguus."⌧ The *DePascha Computus*, an anonymous document believed to have been written in North Africa around 243 CE, placed Jesus birth on March 28. Clement, a bishop of Alexandria (d. ca. 215 CE), thought Jesus was born on November 18. Based on historical records, Fitzmyer guesses that Jesus birth occurred on September 11, 3 BCE."[5]

Other scholars place the birth of Jesus somewhere in late September or early October. Nobody knows for sure, it is only speculation. Nonetheless, we accept Christmas as a Christian holiday and observe it.

Another example is the wearing of wedding bands. So many Christian couples wear wedding bands today as a symbol of their love to each other. The history of the wedding band is not that marvelous either. Scholar Samuele Bacchiocchi at Andrews University has done extensive research in the history and development of finger rings including wedding bands. He found that "the meaning of the wedding ring as a symbol of marital commitment finds its origin not in Scripture, but in pagan mythology and superstitions."[6] Later in the book Bacchiocchi mentions idolatry and other pagan rituals are tied to the wearing of rings and wedding bands. Yet today, we don't think of its origin anymore, but what it symbolizes to the bride and groom. Should we discard the use of the wedding band because the origin was pagan? In the same sense, we cannot discard music just because the origin was pagan or was born outside the church.

6. The drum set and electric guitars are of the devil

The invention of the drum begun in the mid 1800s, not as some Christians believe that it was born in the 1950s along with Rock-N-Roll. Daniel Glass and Vic Firth have done a research on the development of the drum set. According to them, the invention begun in the 1800s when the Civil War was ending and drummers began to experiment by placing more drums around one player to do the

---

5. Origin of Christmas, http://www.simpletoremember.com/vitals/Christmas_TheRealStory.htm,
(accessed 5 March 2015).

6. Samuele Bacchiocchi, *Christian Dress & Adornment*, (Biblical Perspectives, Berrien Springs, MI, 1995) 80.

job of two or three players.[7] Images from the Vic Firth Drumset History Poster show that by 1927 the modern drum set has been established and many drummers were using it. So again, historical facts prove that the drum set was not born in the 1950s as a result of the rock-n-roll revolution, but existed way before. Electric guitar was also born way before the 1950s and way before the rock-n-roll era. It was developed and experimented with in the early 1900s by jazz guitarists who needed louder instruments for their big band ensembles.[8] There is no evidence to support that these instruments were invented by the devil or for devil worship. Drums existed in early cultures after the Creation Week, they were used for different purposes such as music, dance and communication between tribes or on the battle field to give different signals to the soldiers. In the early 1900s however drummers began experimenting for practical purposes. Instead of needing two or three drummers, one could play all those parts easily by combining them into one drum-set. The guitar is the grand-grand-grand baby of the lute from the medieval period. The lute is the grand-grand-grand baby of the lyre that David played. Bach wrote compositions for the lute, Vivaldi wrote composition for the lute, but in those days the calm and soothing sound of the acoustic guitar was sufficiently loud for their small halls. During the big band era where loud instruments surround the guitar, once again out of necessity the acoustic guitar was amplified and turned into an electric instrument to be heard alongside trumpets, trombones and saxophones. Rock musicians simply took advantage of the already existing instruments.

7. Contemporary music plays with the senses and leaves one dry when it's over

Music has the power to touch the senses. There is nothing wrong with that. Other art forms touch the senses as well. Many people

---

7. A Century of Drumming Revolution, http://www.vicfirth.com/drumset-history/, (accessed 5 March 2015).

8. Colin Hempstead and William E. Worthington, *Encyclopedia of 20th-century Technology*, (Routledge Publishing, New York, NY, 2005).

who suffer from low self-esteem, victims of bullying, hurt people, divorced, depressed or lonely, they look to connect emotionally first. These people and others like the homeless, hungry, naked and outcasts need emotional connection and not theological studies. Jesus met people where they were. He was comfortable with that. Generally we are not. We want those people to change their lifestyles, habits, clothes, music, and then come to us and we'll work with them. These people long to hear that someone loves them and cares about them first. Music is an excellent tool for that purpose. God is love. That term is so often used to describe God's character. Love is an emotion; therefore if music draws people to God through emotions and by letting them know that God loves them and cares about them, use it.

8. Many artists in the contemporary Christian world are gossipers and backbiters and compete with each other – these are not Christian values

This again is not a theological or musicological argument. It is an opinion and a judging opinion. Judging others was mentioned earlier in this chapter. I am not defending any artists, and accept the possibility that the argument may be true in some cases, but is that a good reason to discard their music? Once again the words of Jesus come to mind, "And why do you look at the speck in your brother's eye, but do not consider the plank in your own eye?"[9] As an Evangelist and Pastor I had the privilege to travel and serve in many churches in different countries. I have met many Christians and so called-Christians that wore the name, but certainly did not live up to Christian codes or ethics. How many church officers made it to office by stepping on their brethren or spreading rumors about them? How many Christian ladies go to church to compete with their fashion statements or jewelry? Should all these children of God be exiled from the church? Personally when I listen to a song, do not bother investigating the life of the artist.

9. Matthew 7:3 NKJV.

ARGUMENTS

It makes no impact on the music. I like the music. Whether the artist is a backbiter or gossiper or whatever else, it does not show in their music, therefore it does not affect me in any way. If you know something concrete about an artist that is not a rumor or assumption, I recommend the words of Jesus again that was his reply to people who used the same arguments against the scribes and Pharisees, "Therefore whatever they tell you to observe, that observe and do, but do not do according to their works; for they say, and do not do."[10] According to Jesus, these people should not be discarded completely, but listen to what they say, just don't do what they do if the argument is valid.

9. The private life of those musicians is anything but Christian

Once again, who is willing to take the position of a judge? If they do not promote their personal lifestyle in their music, it has no influence on the listener. Keep in mind the we love singing Beethoven's theme from his Ninth Symphony with sacred lyrics, *Joyful, Joyful, We Adore Thee*,[11] yet Beethoven was seen numerous times in public while heavily intoxicated by alcohol. In his study room there were several notes posted on the wall with spiritual inscriptions reminding him to compose only to the glory of God, a task Beethoven was committed to very seriously. Another example is the beautiful hymn we love, *Be Still, My Soul*, by Jean Sibelius.[12] While the original composition was a tone poem and Katharina von Schlegel added sacred lyrics to this beautiful melody, and we love singing it, Sibelius fell victim to alcohol and heavy drinking that ultimately took his life. Yet, we do not discard the beautiful music of Beethoven and Sibelius just because they drank uncontrollably in their private state. Is it fair to keep Beethoven's and

---

10. Matthew 23:3 NKJV.

11. Ludwig van Beethoven, *Melody* from the Ninth Symphony, 1824, lyrics by Henry van Dyke, *Joyful, Joyful, We Adore Thee*, 1907.

12. Jean Sibelius, *Finlandia*, 1899, Katharina von Schlegel, translated by Jane Borthwick, *Be Still, My Soul*, 1855.

Sibelius' music but discard contemporary artists' music for the same reason? Again, as long as these artists do not promote any unchristian views and practices in their music, it does not have any effect on the listener because people like myself do not investigate their private lives prior to listening to their music. If we were to investigate everyone's private life, I wonder how many artists would be worthy to listen to, how many teachers would be worth learning from, how many pastors would be worth hiring, etc. The Bible makes it clear that judgment is God's. I prefer to leave it there.

10. Contemporary Rock music uses rock beat, which is evil because of the syncopation played on the snare drum.

It is true that the snare is played on beats two and four instead of the natural accent of one and three. However, the beat is not only the snare but the bass drum beating the accent on one and three. A rock guitarist I played with several times, told me that he always listened for beat one on the bass rather than the snare. Conclusion, if the snare drum is louder than the rest of the drum rhythm, than it throws the entire song off balance and it is wrong. On the other hand, if the drumbeat is well balanced with the other instruments and the rhythm melts in with the guitars and bass guitar, the heart cannot pick out the syncopation of the drumbeat, but picks up the entire pattern from beat one to four. A well-balanced instrumentation in loudness and rhythm will not increase your blood pressure and your body will not release adrenaline or other harmful chemicals. The issue is not what is played on the drums, but how it is played and how it is balanced with the other instruments of the band.

9

Conclusion
Discerning Good Music from Bad Music

MUSIC IS A CREATION of God and a gift to us to praise God. Everyone is drawn to God differently based on personal state. An introverted person will not praise God as an extraverted person might. A shy person may be more reserved than an outgoing person. The Bible writers counsel us to worship God as we feel in our hearts. Do not copy the person next to you during worship. Express to God the desires of your heart and the feelings of your heart. We have seen Bible passages from Luke and Romans where we are counseled not to judge those around us. The idea is to gather together, praise God for each other – be happy for each other, and ultimately to worship God.

Divisions and discord happens when one generation prefers one style of music and another generation prefers another style of music. Changes ought to be made with much consideration, and with prayer. Both sides need to agree, begin to experiment together and start with small changes to make sure everyone understands and give some time for everyone to get used to it. Big changes made abruptly are dangerous and end with many painful experiences. This is when many leave the church because they feel abandoned or ignored.

If change however is not needed or is not necessary for the local congregation, do not make any changes. If a congregation is happy and satisfied singing Bach chorales, hymns and cantatas, leave things be. If another congregation wants to connect with young people based on the music they listen to, changes are necessary in the selection of music. Today, not many young people are taught to appreciate Bach and other composers in the classical arena. Not long ago I attended a Cleveland Orchestra Concert—a world-renowned orchestra, but as I looked around the attendees, not many young people were present. The majority of attendees were middle-aged to elderly. If we look at how many young people listen to contemporary artists such as Casting Crowns, Chris Tomlin or Skillet to name a few, they are not only drawn because of the music, but because of the freedom they have to express themselves. Even the younger singers who sing with Bill Gaither on his tours are changing their style from the Old Southern Gospels, as we know it to more contemporary expression of their feelings and emotions. They use louder guitars; louder drums and their voices are louder. I wonder what would David say today to people who want to praise God quietly. Again, if the local culture is happy with that and works for the local congregation, keep it. I am just wondering whether David would fit in most of the churches, or would he be a rebel. He praised God with singing, shouting and dancing. Also, what kind of melodies would he use today and how would he beat the drum and the clashing cymbals? Would David use electric instruments or only acoustic ones?

The Azusa Street Mission and Revival used that theology and example of David in their worship in Los Angeles in 1906. They compared their worship to Protestant churches around them that claimed to have encountered God through their spiritual ears, while the people of the Azusa Street Mission professed to encounter God through their spiritual eyes. Their argument is based on Samuel's description that David danced before the Lord,[1] "accompanied by

---

1. See 2 Samuel 6:12–23, 1 Chronicles 15:25–29.

Conclusion

an orchestra of lyres, harps, bronze cymbals, tambourines, trumpets, and castanets. He did not respond to the presence of God in a silent, "reverent," meditative, awe-filled, intellectual mode such as could be found at Los Angele's First Methodist, or First Presbyterian, or First Congregational Church."[2] The author, Cecil M. Robeck argues that David's dance was not only intellectual but emotional, passionate and exuberant. David's dance "was not limited only to his mind. Indeed, it was quite like the worship that many African American slaves enjoyed when left to themselves, with dance and shout, rhythm and song, possession and falling."[3] Robeck continues stating that many people including their pastors did not understand this type of expression of their joy through song and dance, therefore they were despised by many locals, they were publically ridiculed for it and this kept many people from joining or participating in the Azusa Street Mission worship.

Today, many people ridicule, condemn or judge certain types of music without having an understanding of it or keeping in mind that it may help someone connect with God. Just because something does not work for me, it does not mean it cannot work for someone else.

Robeck continues making the point that the people of the Azusa Street Mission did not dance, shout or jump all the time. There were times of silent – reverent moments when people poured out their hearts to God in a kneeling posture, and sometimes at the end of the service people were left speechless when they had the opportunity to express their feelings to God in silence.

I have mentioned earlier in the book that my parents condemned all kinds of music that went beyond classical style and instrumentation including the strumming technique on acoustic guitar. Based on my research not all-Classical music is good, and not all Pop, Rock, Christian Rock is bad. I happened to like classical music, but also like some pop, some rock and some Christian

---

2. Cecil M. Robeck, Jr., *The Azusa Street Mission & Revival; The Birth of the Gobal Pentecostal Movement*, (Nelson Reference & Electronic, Nashville, Tennessee, 2006) 133.

3. Ibid., 133.

rock. What do I base my decision on is very easy. If a particular musical piece or song helps me calm down at the end of the day, or helps me connect with Jesus or draws me closer to Jesus is good music for me. If a particular musical piece or song aggravates me or causes me to be more stressed than I am, that is bad music for me. It is not theologically or musicologically correct to make decisions based on genres. For example I listen to the classical station in my car, but when Halloween comes, they play some very crazy music on the classical station on classical and acoustic instruments. There are plenty of composers in the classical arena that composed music with witchcraft, ghosts, spells and other devilish themes in mind. Are those good music for Christians just because they are played on classical instruments? No. When Halloween comes, I do not listen to the classical station at all. On the other hand, some pop, some rock and some Christian rock is welcomed and appreciated in my book. These are those songs and compositions where the instrumentation is well balanced, one instrument is not dominating over the other and they play in beautiful harmony together with a beautiful melody and creative chord progressions. I do not condemn beautiful folk music or beautiful country music, although I heard the joke that if you listen to country music backwards your dog comes home, your girlfriend comes back and you get your trailer back. I appreciate many country songs that deal with social justice and the artist describes the reality of life.[4] The reason I do not condemn genres in entirety because there are good songs in most of them. For example, one cannot listen to Christian songs in every situation or all aspects of life. I listen to Christian songs throughout the day and while I am driving, but when I dated my wife and after much prayer I was convinced that she was the one for me, I sang to her Paul Anka's *Lonely Boy*. That song is still a favorite on Valentine's Day and other special occasions. If you consider the Songs of Solomon that are part of the Bible, they contain quite graphic lyrics in a dialogue format between Solomon and

---

4. Tex Sample, *Ministry In An Oral Culture; Living With Will Rogers, Uncle Remus & Minnie Pearl*, (Westminster/John Knox Press, Louisville, Kentucky, 1994).

Conclusion

his young bride, the Shulamite Girl. When I want to surprise my wife with a special candle light dinner and music, I will not play *The Old Rugged Cross*, as much as I love that song, but will select a more romantic song to set the atmosphere. One personal favorite selection is Olivia Newton-John's *I honestly love you*, to name an example.

When I got to go through my father's vinyl disc library collection, I made some very surprising discoveries. My father ran the Romanian border in 1985 and we left the country to be with him in the States in 1987, so for almost two years we were without our father at home. As I mentioned earlier, I played many of his discs during the day, as I loved to listen to music. After he left, there were no rules as to what I can listen to or what I can touch because mother was busy bribing government officials to leave us alone and help get the entrance visa to the States as soon as possible. Our family was labeled as deserters in the government's eyes. So one day I decided to go through his entire library to see what other music he had. To my surprise, there were discs with music from the non-classical arena. I began to wonder why my parents only allowed classical music to be played in the house, but in my father's collection there was a disc by Willie Nelson, another one by Olivia Newton-John (that is when I first heard the song *I honestly love you*), and other pop artists. Apparently my father enjoyed some pop music himself, but perhaps kept it a secret because of the church's position on the matter?

Music is a gift from God. There is no doubt the devil tries to use it to drive people away from God, but there is still good music out there. I recommend the same measuring rod for your musical selection. If the music brings you closer to God and into a stronger and a more loving relationship with your Savior, use it, listen to it sing it and play it on your instruments. If on the other hand it causes division, harm or any other negative effect to you and those around you, do not listen to it, do not sing it, and do not play it. Rob Vandeman was right when he stated in that article quoted earlier that some of the music played on that radio station is not for his taste, but if it helps reach commuters and bring them into a closer walk with Jesus, it is worth having it. There are Christian contemporary songs that are way over my understanding and tolerable hearing range, but if it helps others get closer to Jesus, who am I to judge?

My old professor of music history had a very interesting comment after reading Aranza's book on *Backward Masking Unmasked*. In his opinion music has the power to bring to surface whatever is inside you. I agree with my professor based on an experiment conducted on my parishioners. A Biblical passage was given for a five-minute meditation. During those five minutes nobody was allowed to talk or share his/her findings. After the five minutes of meditation everyone had to write down personal impressions of that particular Biblical passage. It was interesting to hear the results. Everyone read and meditated on the very same passage, but the optimistic ones became more optimistic and the pessimistic ones became more pessimistic. The same experiment could be conducted with music, but the point ought to be made that this experiment is valid with only randomly selected songs or instrumental pieces that do not contain lyrics. A discouraged person may become more discouraged while listening to the same music; an energetic person may become more energetic. If music is selected carefully and cautiously and only positive and uplifting music is selected, the thoughts may be raised in praise and adoration to God who created music and gave it to us as another means for us to stay connected with heaven. If on the other hand a group or individual musicians openly confess to be Satan worshippers and promote the same in their music and their concerts, that music ought to be discarded immediately by Christians who desire to serve God regardless of instrumentation, rhythm, melody, chord progression, etc.

Heaven is our final destiny, and as music helped many struggling people in bondage, slavery and oppression make it through, may music help us make it into God's Kingdom. There we will continue singing, playing harps and praising God with the Redeemed and the angelic hosts throughout the ceaseless years of eternity. John recorded in the book of Revelation, "they sing the song of

Conclusion

Moses, the servant of God, and the song of Lamb, . . ."[5] That is certainly something to look forward to.

May God give us the wisdom we need to make our musical selections in such a way, that they would draw us closer to our Savior and Redeemer, Jesus Christ. The Apostle Paul counsels us, "And do not be drunk with wine, in which is dissipation; but be filled with the Spirit, speaking to one another in psalms and hymns and spiritual songs, singing and making melody in your heart to the Lord, giving thanks always for all things to God the Father in the name of our Lord Jesus Christ, submitting to one another in the fear of God."[6]

---

5. Revelation 15:3 NKJV.
6. Ephesians 5:18–21 NKJV.

Bibliography

Achtemeier, Paul J., Green, Joel B. and Thompson, Marianne Meye. *Introducing the New Testament; Its Literature and Theology*. Michigan: William B. Eerdmans Publishing Company, 2001.
Ancient Jewish Lyre. Accessed March 25, 2013. http://www.ancientjewishlyre.com.
Aranza, Jacob, *Backward Masking Unmasked*, Shreveport, LA: Huntington House, Inc, 1984.
Arnold, Bill T. *1 & 2 Samuel; The NIV Application Commentary*. Michigan: Zondervan, 2003.
Attridge, Harold W. *Fully Revised & Updated The Harper Collins Study Bible; Including Apocryphal Deuterocanonical Books; New Revised Standard Version*. Harper Collins Publishers, 1989.
Bacchiocchi, Samuele. *Christian Dress & Adornment*. Berrien Springs, MI: Biblical Perspectives, 1995.
Bainbridge, William Sims. *The Sociology of Conversion; In Handbook of Religious Conversion*. Alabama: Religious Education Press, 1992.
Bede, Venerable. *The Ecclesiastical History of the English People*. Oxford: Oxford University Press, 1994.
Beethoven, Ludwig van. Melody from the Ninth Symphony, 1824. Lyrics by Henry van Dyke, *Joyful, Joyful, We Adore Thee*, 1907.
Begbie, Jeremy S. *The Beauty of God: Theology and the Arts*. Illinois: InterVarsity Press, 2007.
Berdyaev, Nicolas. *The Meaning of the Creative Act*. London: Victor Gollancz, 1955.
Blickenstaff, Marianne. *While the Bridegroom is with them; Marriage, Family, Gender and Violence in the Gospel of Matthew*. New York: T&T Clark International, 2005.
Blume, Friedrich. *Protestant Church Music*. London: Victor Gollancz, 1975.
Bodner, Keith. *1 Samuel; A Narrative Commentary*. Tennessee: Sheffield Phoenix Press, 2008.

Bibliography

Boyd Brown, Christopher. *Singing the Gospel; Lutheran Hymns and the Success of the Reformation*. Massachusetts: Harvard University Press, 2005.

Buckser, Andrew and Glazier, Stephen D. *The Anthropology of Religious Conversion*. Maryland: Rowman and Littlefield Publishers Inc., 2003.

Calvin, John. *Institutes of the Christian Religion II*. Maryland: Westminster Press, 1960.

Campbell, Antony F. *1 Samuel; The forms of the Old Testament Literature*. William B. Eerdmans Publishing Company, Michigan, 2003Cartledge, Tony W. *1 & 2 Samuel: Smyth & Helwys Bible Commentary*. Georgia: Smyth & Helwys, 2001

Cheyne, T.K. and Black, J.S. *Encyclopaedia Biblica*. Massachusetts: Norwood Press, 1899.

Child. Accessed February 28, 2013. http://www.merriamwebster.com/dictionary/child.

Conversion. Accessed November 14, 2013. http://www.merriam-webster.com/dictionary/conversion.

Crowley, Aleister. *Magick*. Massachusetts: Red Wheel/Weiser, 1913.

———. *The Confessions of Aleister Crowley: An Autohagiography*. New York: Arkana Publishing, 1989.

Crowley, Gary. *Band Explosion*. Accessed June 19, 2011. http://www.imdb.com/title/tt1948261/.

De Gruchy, John W. *Christianity, Art and Transformation: Theological Aesthetics in the Struggle of Justice*. New York: Cambridge University Press, 2003.

Devil Worship: Exposing Satan's Underground. Accessed October 3, 2013. http://www.imdb.com/title/tt1136645/.

Dillenberger, John *A Theology of Artistic Sensibilities: The Visual Arts and the Church*. London: Student Christian Movement, 1987.

Douglas, Mary. *Purity and Danger*. New York: Published by Routledge, 1966.

Ellwood, Robert S. Jr. *One Way: The Jesus Movement and Its Meaning*. Englewood Cliffs: Prentice-Hall, Inc., 1973.

Firth, David G. *1 & 2 Samuel; Apollos Old Testament Commentary*. Illinois: Intervarsity Press, 2009.

Flannery, Austin. *Vatican Council II: Constitutions, Decrees, Declarations*. New York: Costello Publishing Company, 1996.

France, R.T. *The Gospel of Matthew: The New International Commentary on the New Testament*. Grand Rapids, MI: William B. Eerdmans Publishing Company, 2007.

Frost, Michael. *The Road to Missional; Journey to the Center of the Church*. Michigan: BakerBooks, 2011.

Geraldo Rivera on Satanism. Accessed November 19, 2012. http://io9.com/582971/when-geraldo-rivera-took-on-satanism-and-a-very-confused-ozzy-osbourne.

Gonzalez, Justo L. *The Story of Christianity; The Early Church to the Dawn of the Reformation*, New York: HarperCollins, 2010, Vol. 1.

BIBLIOGRAPHY

Gorringe, Tim. *Renbrandt's Religious Art, Theology.* 98 (1995): 15f.

Grenz, Stanley J. *Theology for the Community of God.* Michigan: William G. Eerdmans Publishing Company, 2000.

Grout, Donald Jay and Palisca, Claude V. *A History of Western Music.* New York: W.W. Norton & Company, New York, 1988.

Hagner, Donald A. *Word Biblical Commentary, Volume 33b: Matthew 14–28.* Nelson Reference & Electronic: A Division of Thomas Nelson Publishers, 1995.

Hamel, Paul. *The Christian and his Music.* Washington D.C.: Review and Herald Publishing Association, 1973.

Hauerwas, Stanley. *Matthew; Brazos Theological Commentary on the Bible.* Michigan: Brazos Press, 2006.

Harp and Lyre. Accessed March 25, 2013. http://www.jewishencyclopedia.com/articles/7266-harp-and-lyre.

Hart, David Bentley. *Beauty of the Infinite.* Michigan: William B. Eerdmans Publishing Company, 2004.

Hempstead, Colin and William E. Worthington, *Encyclopedia of 20th-century Technology.* New York: Routledge Publishing, 2005.

Hervieu-Leger, Daniele. *Religion as a Chain of Memory.* New Jersey: Rutgers University Press, 2000.

Hirsch, Alan. *The Forgotten Ways.* Michigan: Brazos Press, 2006.

Imaging the Word: An Arts and Lectionary Resource. Volume 2. Ohio: United Church Press, 1995.

Indignant. Accessed February 28, 2013. http://www.merriam-webster.com/dictionary/indignant.

Infant. Accessed February 28, 2013. http://www.merriamwebster.com/dictionary/infant.

Jimmy Page on e owned Aleister Crowley's former home. Accessed October 3, 2013.

http:www.rollingstone.com/music/lists/the-10-wildest-led-zeppelin-legends-fact-checked-20121121/jimmy-page-once-owned-aleister-crowleys-former-home-19691231.

Johnson, Carolyn Y. *Science in Mind; Is the person you are today the real, final You?*

Harvard study says you'll change more than you think. Boston Globe Newspaper, 2013.

Jowett, Benjamin. *The Republic of Plato.* Oxford Clarendon Press, 1888.

Keller, Timothy. *Center Church.* Michigan: Zondervan, 2012.

Kellerman, James A. quoting Homily. *Ancient Christian Texts; Incomplete Commentary on Matthew (Opus Imperfectum).* Illinois: Intervarsity Press, 2010.

Kinnaman, David. *You Lost Me. Why Young Christians Are Leaving Church... And Rethinking Faith.* Michigan: Baker Books, 2011.

——— and Gabe Lyons. *unchristian; What a New Generation Really Thinks About Christianity... And Why It Matters.* Michigan: Baker Books, 2007.

Bibliography

Kroeger Catherine Clark & Evans, Mary J. *The IVP Women's Bible Commentary.* Illinois: Intervarsity Press, 2002.

Lawson, Kim Dr. *Ministry with People with Disabilities; Emphasis on Alzheimer's Disease."* Lecture given at United Theological Seminary Intensive Week, Dayton, OH, January 31, 2015.

Luther, Martin. *Geystliche Gesangk Buchleyn.* Wittenberg, 1524, LW 53:315–16.

Macchia, Frank D. *Baptized in the Spirit.* Michigan: Zondervan, 2006.

Maynard-Reid, Pedrito U. *Diverse Worship; African-American, Caribbean & Hispanic Perspectives.* Illinois: Inter Varsity Press, 2000.

Meintel, Deirdre. *When There Is No Conversion: Spiritualists and Personal Religious Change.* Anthropologica 49 (1): 149–62. Canada: Universite de Montreal, 2007.

Mellish, Kevin J. *1 & 2 Samuel; A Commentary in the Wesleyan Tradition.* Kansas City: Beacon Hill Press, 2012.

Moltmann, Jurgen. *The Source of Life.* Minnesota: Fortress Press, 1997.

Motorhead Music. Accessed October 3, 2013. http://www.sing365.com/music/Lyrics.nsf/Don't- Need-Religion-lyrics-Motorhead/D04CD4168806725948256C55000C55DF.

Murphy, Francesca Aran. *1 Samuel.* Michigan: Brazos Press, 2010.

New Orleans Music History. Accessed October 3, 2013. http://www.neworleansonline.com/neworleans/music/musichistory.

Noll, Mark A. and Blumhofer, Edith L. *Sing Them Over Again to Me; Hymns And Hymnbooks in America.* University of Alabama Press, Tuscaloosa, 2006.

Noll, Mark A. and Blumhofer, Edith L. *Sing Them Over Again to Me: Hymns and Hymnbooks in America.* Tuscaloosa: The University of Alabama Press, 2006.

Nolland, John. *The Gospel of Matthew; A Commentary on the Greek Text.* Grand Rapids, MI: William B. Eerdmans Publishing Company, 2005.

O'Leary, Ann M. *Matthew's Judaization of Mark; Examined in the Context of the Use of Sources in Graeco-Roman Antiquity.* London: T & T Clark, 2006.

Origin of Christmas. http://www.simpletoremember.com/vitals/Christmas_TheRealStory.htm. Accessed 5 March 2015.

Osborne, Grant R. *Matthew; Exegetical Commentary on the New Testament.* Michigan: Zondervan, 2010.

Otto, Rudolf. *The IDEA of the HOLY.* Oxford University Press, 1950.

Palisca, Claude V. *Norton Anthology of Western Music.* Fourth Edition. New York: W.W. Norton & Company, 2001.

Pregeant, Russell. *Matthew; Chalice Commentaries for TODAY.* Missouri: Chalice Press, 2004.

Randel, Don Michael. *The New Harvard Dictionary of Music.* Massachusetts: The Belknap Press of Harvard University Press, 1986.

Regamey, Pie-Raymond. *Religious Art in the Twentieth Century.* New York: Herder and Herder, 1963.

BIBLIOGRAPHY

Religious Conversion. Accessed November 14, 2013. http://www.princeton.edu/-achaney/tmve/wiki100k/docs/Religious, conversion.
Robeck, Cecil M. Jr. *The Azusa Street; Mission & Revival; The Birth of the Global Pentecostal Movement.* Nashville: Thomas Nelson Publishers, 2006.
Rossing, Thomas D. *The Science of Sound.* New York: Addison-Wesley Publishing Company, 1990.
Roxburgh, Alan J. *Missional; Joining God in the Neighborhood.* Michigan: Baker Books, 2011.
Sample, Tex. *White Soul; Country Music, the Church and Working Americans.* Nashville: Abingdon Press, 1996.
———. *Ministry in an Oral Culture; Living with Will Rogers, Uncle Remus, & Minnie Pearl.* Kentucky: Westminster/John Knox Press, 1994.
Seventh-day Adventists Believe; An exposition of the fundamental beliefs of the Seventh-day Adventist Church. Idaho: Pacific Press Publishing Association, 2005.
Seventh-day Adventist Fundamental Beliefs. As voted during the Annual Council of the General Conference Executive Committee on Sunday, September 27, 1998, in Iguacu Falls, Brazil.
Seventh-day Adventist Minister's Handbook. Maryland: Prepared and Published by The Ministerial Association of The General Conference of Seventh-day Adventists. 1997.
Sibelius, Jean. *Finlandia.* 1899, Katharina von Schlegel, translated by Jane Borthwick, *Be Still, My Soul,* 1855.
Simonetti, Maulio quoting Hilary of Poitiers. *Ancient Christian Commentary on Scripture.* Illinois: Intervarsity Press, 2002.
Slaughter, Mike. *Spiritual Entrepreneurs.* Tennessee: Abingdon Press, 1994.
Slave trade and music. Accessed October 3, 2013. http://www.soundjunction.org/howtheslavetradeaffectedmusicanintroduction.aspa.
Stark, Rodney. *Becoming a World-Saver; American Sociological Review.* New Jersey: Harper Collins and Princeton University Press, 1965.
———. *The Rise of Christianity; How the Obscure, Marginal Jesus Movement Because the Dominant Religious Force in the Western World In a Few Centuries.* New Jersey: Harper Collins and Princeton University Press, 1966.
Stern. Accessed February 28, 2013. http://www.merriam-webster.com/dictionary/stern.
Stolba, Marie K. *The Development of Western Music; A History.* Wisconsin: WCB Brown & Benchmark Publishers, 1990.
Streiker, Lowell D. *The Jesus Trip: Advent of the Jesus Freaks.* Nashville: Abingdon, 1971.
Strodach, Paul Zeller. *Luther's Works: Liturgy and Hymns.* Volume 53. Philadelphia: Fortress Press, 1965.
Sullivan, Mark. *"'More Popular Than Jesus': The Beatles and the Religious Far Right" Popular Music.* Article 6 (3): 313–26, 1987.

BIBLIOGRAPHY

Swatos, William H. Jr. *Encyclopedia of Religion and Society.* Pennsylvania: Alta Mira Press, 1998.

Tanis, James R. *Seeing Beyond the World: Visual Arts and the Calvinist Tradition.* Michigan: Eerdmans Publishing, 1999.

Tennent, Timothy C. *Invitation to World Missions; A Trinitarian Missiology for the Twenty-first Century.* Michigan: Kregel Publications, 2010.

Thiessen, Gesa Elsbeth. *Theological Aesthetics: A Reader.* Grand Rapids, MI: William B. Eerdmans Publishing Company, 2004.

Torres, Louis R. & Carol A. Torres. *Notes on Music,* St. Maries, ID: LMN Publishing International, Inc., 1996.

Tsumura, David Toshio. *The First Book of Samuel.* Michigan: William B. Eerdmans Publishing Company, 2007.

Turner, David L. *Matthew: Baker Exegetical Commentary on the New Testament.* Grand Rapids, MI: Baker Publishing Group, 2008.

Tyson, John R. *Assist me to Proclaim; The life and hymns of Charles Wesley.* Michigan: William B. Eerdmans Publishing Company, 2007.

United Church Press. *Imaging the Word: An Arts and Lectionary Resource, Volume 2.* Cleveland: United Church Press, 1995.

Vandeman, Rob. *Music Can Change the World,* article for the Visitor magazine. Nampa, ID: Pacific Press Publishing Association, February issue, 2015.

Vatican Council II: Constitutions, Decrees, Declarations, ed. Austin Flannery. New York: Costello Publishing Company, 1996.

Watkins, Keith. *A Few Kind Words for Fanny Crosby.* Worship 51, no. 3 (May 1977): 248–59.

Warner, Stephen R., Nancy T. Ammerman, Jackson W. Carroll, Carl S. Dudley, Nancy L. Eiesland, William McKinney, Robert L. Schreiter, Scott L. Thumma. *Studying Congregations; A New Handbook.* Nashville: Abingdon Press, 1998.

Westrup, J.A. and Harrison, F.L.I. *The New College Encyclopedia of Music.* New York: W.W. Norton & Company, Inc., 1981.

White, Ellen G. *Pastoral Ministry,* Maryland: Ministerial Association General Conference of Seventh-day Adventists, 1995.

Wilkins, Michael J. *Matthew: The NIV Application Commentary.* Michigan: Zondervan, 2004.

Wilson-Dickson, Andrew. *The Story of Christian Music; From Gregorian Chant to Black Gospel.* Minnesota: Fortress Press, 2003.

Witherington, Ben. *Matthew; Smyth & Helwys Bible Commentary.* Smyth & Helwys Georgia: Publishing Incorporated, 2006.

Wolff, Christoph. *Johann Sebastian Bach.* New York: W.W. Norton and Company, 2000.

Wycliffe, John. *Sermon on the Feigned Contemplative Life.* London: Hope Pub Co, 1967.

Zacharias, Ravi. *Has Christianity Failed You?* Michigan: Zondervan, 2010.